# KABIR

## SEVEN HUNDRED SAYINGS

### Versions by Paul Smith

**N-B**

## New Humanity Books

KABIR ... SEVEN HUNDRED SAYINGS

NEW HUMANITY BOOKS
83 BOURKE STREET
MELBOURNE VICTORIA 3000
AUSTRALIA

First Edition 1988

ISBN   0 949191 01 9

Front cover design and other designs in this book
are of Indian cotton print patterns.

Thanks go to my wife, Ann, for editing this book.

Dedicated to Adi K. Irani, a great friend and helper.

Printed in Singapore by Tien Wah Press.

# Introduction

Kabir (meaning 'great') was born near Varanasi (Banaras), India, in 1398 A.D. and died towards the end of the 15th Century. He was brought up by an elderly Muslim weaver-couple named Niru and Nima, having been abandoned shortly after birth. He learnt the same trade as his new parents and used the imagery of weaving often in his poems.

It is said that he had a number of Gurus or spiritually perfected Masters. One was a Sufi Master named Shekh Taqqi. The most famous was Ramanand. Kabir wanted to become his disciple, but it was said that Ramanand only accepted Brahmins as disciples. Kabir refused to accept this. He devised a plan! One day he hid under the steps of the ghats where Ramanand would go to bathe early every morning. Ramanand stepped on the body of Kabir (as Kabir had hoped). The Master having trod on one of God's creatures called out "Ram, Ram", his personal mantra or prayer to God. Kabir, having obtained the prayer began to recite it and Ramanand on seeing the sincerity and cleverness of the young man accepted him as a disciple.

Kabir strongly denounced the orthodox ways of religions: rituals and ceremonies. His quick wit and razor sharp tongue tore strips off the hypocritical theologians and priests.

He proved to the people through the pure logic of the heart the stupidity of believing that religions are different from each other by pointing out the essential sameness in all of them.

At a time when the Muslims and Hindus were at each others throats this was a very brave thing to do, and by doing it he brought an end to their fighting.

After many years his Master gave him the experience of God-consciousness and perfected him. Kabir became a Perfect Master himself, experiencing being God and man simultaneously.

In many of his poems he tells of this experience and teaches us that we too are inwardly God and have only to pray to God, follow a True Master, love our fellow creatures and above all, be honest, to experience this same Self within all of us.

Kabir's short teaching poems which are called Sakhis (meaning 'sayings' or 'witness') are like short, hard, sharp punches at the heart – direct, full of force, they take your breath away for a moment, you see stars, they hurt for quite some time afterwards, they are a real shock to the system, to the intellect, the dishonesty we nurture inside ourselves.

Here is the Truth told with no frills or compromises, The patient is dying – so cut out the cancer of the ego. Cut, cut, deeper and deeper, cut it away and stop it from spreading.

Here are wonderful words of wisdom from one of the wisest of the wise.

Here are lines of love from a Master of Divine Love, and a human being who has lived as all human beings should live, with compassion, honesty and courage.

If you want the Truth, no holds barred, it is here, but as we are told: Truth is a dangerous thing! These poems change people. You will not be the same! You will be a loser! But, what you will lose was never worth keeping anyway – and what you will gain will be a treasure worth keeping more than all the gold that ever existed. As Kabir says: "wake up, sleepy head!"

These versions were composed from the translations listed in the bibliography. I have kept as close to the original rhyme-structure as I could. A rhyme helps to keep the meaning in the memory – that's why songs are popular.

Thanks go out to all the authors who have written works on Kabir and to those who translated his poems: without them this book could not have happened. Thanks also to Clarice Adams for the typing and to my wife, Ann, for the editing. And, of course, to the One in us all.

Paul Smith

4

# GLOSSARY

HARI: God.

RAM: The Avatar, Messiah, First Perfect Master Who incarnates periodically: Adam, Zoroaster, Rama, Krishna, Buddha, Jesus, Mohammed, Meher Baba. God in human form and God beyond human form. The Divine Name.

MAYA: Illusion, false attachment. Ignorance's root. God's shadow.

MANTRA: A sacred name or phrase given by a Master to a disciple.

GURU: A spiritual teacher or Master. Kabir often talks of true (Perfect) Masters and false masters.

PERFECT MASTER: The God-realized human being. The true Teacher: Ramanand, Kabir, Moses, John the Baptist, Francis of Assissi, Hafiz, Rumi, Ramakrishna, Sai Baba etc.

LAKE MANSAROVER: A lake at the foot of Kailas peak. Literally, the Lake of the Mind.

VEDIC RITES: Ancient Indian rituals.

HUSBAND: God or the Perfect Master.

WIFE: Disciple.

YAMA: Hindu god of death.

THE WORD: God's Name. The Ultimate Truth. Ram.

KALI: Hindu goddess of destruction.

BRAHMA: The Creator.

SHIVA: The Destroyer.

KAABA: The shrine in Mecca to which all Muslims pray.

SAINT: Sometimes Kabir talks about true Saints (God-advanced souls) and sometimes false saints.

SADHU: A pilgrim. An advanced soul.

PUNDIT: Scholar, teacher, professor.

# BIBLIOGRAPHY

Jhabvala, S.H.   KABIR Translated from Original Hindi into English
Bombay (date?)

Prem Chand,   A translation of Kabir's complete Bijak into English
Calcutta, 1911.

Ahmed Shah,   The Bijak of Kabir   Hamipur, 1917 Republished by
Asian Publication Services, New Delhi 1977.

Trumpp, E.,   THE ADI-GRANTH   London, 1877. Trumpp's translation
includes some of Kabir's poems that are in THE ADI-GRANTH.

Lala Kanoo Lal,   One hundred and seventy-five Moral Sayings of
Kabir selected and translated into English   Madras, 1923.

Tagore, Rabindratnath,   One Hundred Poems of Kabir   with an
Introduction by Miss E. Underhill, London, 1914.

Macve, Prabhakar,   Kabir   with a foreword by H.P. Dvenedi,
Sahitya Akademi, New Delhi 1968. 59 page sel. of Kabir's poems.

Uniyal, J.P.,   KABIR   New Delhi, 1968.

Ezekiel, Isaac A.,   Kabir The Great Mystic   Radha Soami Satsang
Beas, Punjab, India. 3rd ed. 1978. 340 pages.

Bly, Robert,   The Kabir Book - Forty-Four of the Ecstatic Poems
of Kabir   Beacon Press  -  Boston 1977. Modern interpretations
using Tagore's translations.

Vaudeville, Ch.,   Kabir   Oxford, 1974 340 pages.

Westcott, G.H.,   Kabir and the Kabir Panth   1907; Susil Gupta Ltd.
1965. India.

Dwyer, SJ. William J.   BHAKTI IN KABIR   Associated Book Agency.
Patna, India. 1981

Behari, B.   Sufis, Mystics and Yogis of India   ed. K.M. Munshi,
Bombay, Bharatiya Vidya Bhavan, 1962. Trans. of Kabir's poems:
pages 221-252.

Hari Prasad Shastri,   INDIAN MYSTIC VERSE   Shanti Sadan, London
1941, 1963. pages 37-55.

The nearest relative one has is the Master;
awakening of spirit is a gift: none greater.
No greater giver of Gifts exists than Hari,
His servants haven't equal in a community.

Sixty-four large lamps may be burning bright
and fourteen moons inside might give light,
but moonlight won't exist in the slightest
where Perfect Master finds no home to rest.

Darkness of night was meant to be abolished
by eighty-four hundred million moons passed:
but without the true Guru they came, went,
still blind, though many lives they spent!

What is possible for that poor Guru to do
if the disciple's at fault and not the Guru?
Guru tries to wake him but without success
for Guru blows in bamboo, a waste I confess.

If the so called 'guru' cannot see well then
his disciple is blind from birth: and when
those who are blind lead those who are blind
and both in a hole fall, both you won't find.

All the world has been eaten by great Doubt
but none have eaten Doubt, inside or out:
only a few who felt Guru's Word in heart
have eaten up Doubt, after tearing it apart.

Let the Perfect Master burn everything away
using Wisdom as tool: let Guru have his way;
with the Word as scraper let him be scraping
and let soul be a mirror from his polishing.

The true Hero is really the Perfect Master,
who let fly arrow, a Word: the Great Archer.
I fell on the dirt as soon as target was hit,
and a deep wound opened after receiving it.

I was saved when I was about to be drowned
by whim of Guru, by whose wave I surfed:
I witnessed the old form, the boat, shatter,
and I was saved when of 'me' I jumped clear.

Stability and salvation were found by me
when the Guru set me in the Source, firmly:
Kabir, the Diamond of Reality can be bought
on bank of Lake Mansarover if It's sought.

I could no longer speak and I was senseless
and my ears could no longer hear, I confess;
for legs to move was no longer a possibility
when arrow of the Master deeply pierced me

Infinite is the Glory of the Perfect Master
and also his Grace, for he's the great Giver;
eyes were opened to Infinity by his Grace
and I then saw beyond all time and space.

I was slowly following in the world's wake
and following Vedic rites, for their sake,
the on the path the Perfect Guru met me
and in my hand he put a lamp so I could see.

Lamp full of oil to me the true Guru gave,
its wick won't dry up, oil one needn't save:
as far as I feel, all bartering is finished,
no longer I'll go to world to be replenished.

When you find Guru who is the Wisdom-giver
will you wander from such a One? Never!
For it's only through Grace of great Govind
that the true Guru you will seek and find.

You have found the Master: but what then
if your mind's still full of mistakes? When
cloth has been soiled and spoiled already,
coming to poor red dye what fate shall be?

I give myself to Guru in sacrifice each day,
at least a hundred times a day in each way:
the true Guru made God from a man like me
and it took no time, all time ceased to be.

Myself to Perfect Master I've offered again,
with all the sincerity my heart can contain:
this, the Age of Death, vainly attacked me
because my determination went on endlessly.

The Perfect Master placed bow in his hand
and let fly his arrows at where I did stand,
one arrow which with his Love he had fired
wounded me ceaselessly: my heart pierced.

No longer able to laugh or to talk at all,
changeable mind is finished, beyond recall!
Kabir says that it often stabbed me through,
that sharp weapon, that Word of the Guru.

The Perfect Guru fits arrow then lets fly,
he keeps arm steady with his watchful eye:
my Guru's arrow did hit my poor naked form
and the Forest burst into a blazing storm.

Kabir, when the Perfect Master I've found,
salt vanished, into the flour it was ground:
disappeared have caste, lineage and family,
and so what name then can you give to me?

Finding Guru is the greatest benefit for you,
alone you are lost, I Kabir, say this is true.
It's like a moth that's drawn to lamp's fire,
it knows its fate and falls to its desire.

Maya's like the lamp and the moth is man;
circling it, man falls: won't stop if he can.
Kabir says, it's only due to wisdom of Guru
that some are saved from Maya, though few.

Seated on platform of Divine Consciousness
the Master gave to me the gift of firmness:
now liberated from all doubt and all fear
the only One Who Exists is adored by Kabir.

The true Guru and Govind are but only One,
and all who exist are but rays of that Sun:
by annihilating the self and adoring Hari,
Divine Vision man is granted so he can See.

Kabir, they haven't found the Perfect Master
and only know half, remain none the wiser:
dressed in robes of the wandering ascetic,
door to door they beg, they are so pathetic.

Perfect Master is my Hero: Kabir's no liar!
Like blacksmith, he keeps iron in the fire:
he made it pure and into gold he made it,
its essence he extracted by the fire he lit.

With patience and consistency Guru gave me
that everlasting Treasure of the Reality:
many farmers would like a crop like this,
but Kabir won't share It, for It is now his.

At intersection is laid out the dice-board
in market that goes up, down: none scored.
When you have as your partner the Master,
it's impossible in this game to be the loser.

By his taking up the dice that's called Love,
by making the board from his bodily glove,
learning from the Master all about the throw
servant Kabir played from the first "go".

When I had found Grace with the True Guru
to me he made a revelation ‘unique and true,
then poured out upon me the cloud of Love
and my body was fully soaked from up above.

When the snake of separation is in the body
no ritual word can control or set it free:
whoever is separated from Ram won't survive
but if he survives, he'll be mad, if alive.

The body was entered by snake of separation
and the heart felt its fangs of separation,
yes, not one movement the snake does make,
saying: "Bite as you like, more I can take."

In sky, Kunjha cranes make mournful cries:
thunder is heard, lakes fill from the skies,
but one who has been deserted by her Lord
suffers torment that can't be told by word.

All night the Lakvi bird is alone, agitated,
at day's break she and her mate are united;
but ones who from Ram are always distant,
not day nor night is He found for an instant.

In separation from Ocean (the Pearl Giver)
oh conch shell wait, don't yet be lamenter;
you will have to cry out in all the shrines
when the Sun rises and upon you it shines.

Inside the heart there burns a large fire,
yet no smoke is seen, but fire grows higher:
he who it burns away that flame does know,
and he also knows He Who did make it grow.

In the fires of separation the log that's wet
smoulders, smokes and spits where it's set:
from separation it will never find a way out
until it becomes ashes: that, do not doubt.

She who is in separation stands, falls again
and again, desiring to see You, great Ram!
If You give her Insight after she has died
what use is it when she's on the other side?

11

After death comes please don't let us meet
oh Ram, this Kabir prays: a prayer complete!
When into dust becomes that old rusted iron,
what can be done by Philosopher's Stone?

He will surely die, that one who is wounded.
even if the knife of separation is blunted:
he then lies down under the tree, moaning;
will it be today or tomorrow he'll be dying?

On the water the blazing fires of separation
burnt away all slime and rotten vegetation,
and all the theologians from South and North
died while they were pondering its worth.

Physician, go home and look after yourself,
you can do nothing, so see to your health:
the One causing disease that hurts so much,
only He can cure disease, His Grace is such.

No relief day or night for this separation,
even while dreaming there's no liberation:
Kabir says, one who is separated from Ram
finds no help is sunshine or shade's calm.

Do not heap abuse upon that separated one,
for that one is a King, though in a dungeon.
A body that doesn't feel pangs of separation
stays forever a place for fiery annihilation.

Body is the lute and veins are the strings,
separation plays endlessly on both and sings;
but this music can be heard by not anyone,
only by the soul and God, the **Supreme** One.

I've been waiting, waiting for so many days
Ram, I've searched the road **and** the ways:
to meet You my heart is **longing,** is longing,
still there is no peace my soul is knowing.

Away my great despair will never be going
if it is only a message that I am hearing,
it will only leave when Hari comes to me
or when I am finally allowed to go to Hari.

I will burn away this form of mine to ashes
so that to the sky much smoke then rises:
isn't it possible that then Hari will pity
me and to quench that fire will rain on me.

This body I will burn away to make the ink;
I'll make a pen from my bones, ink to drink:
and then I'll write the great Name of Ram,
and my letter I will then send to Lord Ram.

In the great pain of Love eyes are washed
and all think they hurt from being diseased,
but it is from crying for Ram, my Lover,
that to everyone they look red and tender.

I wandered far from mountain to mountain,
eyes were ruined by tears they did contain;
but that Herb that heals I never discovered,
Herb that meant my life would be recovered.

These eyes have become completely insane
because they desire to see You again, again:
I didn't find You and I didn't find happiness
and all I have gained is despair in excess.

In the water is where the blue lotus stays
and in the sky the moon is staying, always;
yet One Who is the One Who one loves, He
is forever remaining here! Can't you see?

If the **true Guru** is staying north in Varanasi
and if disciple is staying south by the sea,
**still the** separation does not really exist
for as long as disciple's worth does persist.

13

That One Who is the One that one is loving
will one way or another, closer be coming:
from that One to Whom one gave body, soul,
on trust, impossible to part: part or whole!

Only one mind exists for disciple and Master
for mind's merged with Mind: praise merger!
Master is not happy if cleverness is shown,
only if sincerity in the disciple has grown.

On the path stands the lonely wife, waiting,
suddenly she runs to the traveller, asking:
"Tell me, give me some news of my Husband,
when will He come, return to this land?"

It's surely impossible for me to come to You
and to make You come here's impossible too:
You'll take my life away from me this way,
burning it all away in separation all day.

Kabir, I am suffering deeply, so completely
that from this cage, pain is never set free:
this agony of love, unlike anything at all,
into core of my being cut, past every wall.

Wound that separation causes is so complete
that total destruction the body does meet:
the One Who strikes, alone knows suffering;
except for one who suffering is enduring.

Both eyes have become sore and weakened
from always looking out at the road's end;
all over my tongue the blisters can be seen,
because constantly crying for Ram I've been.

Husband can't be enticed by soul's laughter;
only ones to meet Him are ones who suffer:
if one found Beloved by being happy or gay,
from deserted wife Husband won't stay away.

Kabir, day went by while she was waiting
and the night has slowly away been passing:
one who is separated does not her Lord meet
but spends her life in torment and defeat.

Let that one who is separated pass away
or else reveal Yourself to that one today!
This burning that seems to go on forever
is impossible for Kabir to bear any longer.

The body and soul were burnt to extinction
in that great blazing inferno of separation:
the suffering is no longer felt by the dead,
it's only that Fire that by that pain is fed.

Kabir, it was during a dream I met Hari
and from my sleep He roused and woke me:
now I am terrified that if I close my eyes
then like a dream goes away, away He flies.

Good qualities of my Lord beyond counting,
in my heart are written in large lettering:
to drink some water now I would not dare,
I'm frightened they'd wash away from there.

Kabir, listen to the young wife crying out:
"Spouse, listen;" crying, she does shout:
"Come to my side, come here, come quickly,
or life I'll give up, I'll let it leave me."

Kabir, either that one love has never tasted
or, after, its flavour he has not enjoyed:
like one visiting a house, finding emptiness
leaves it, being unchanged: not more or less.

Within my eyes come, so I then may gaze
upon You all through the nights and days.
Let it soon be that the day will come to me
when sight of Him is given by great Hari!

From my eyes a raging torrent does spray,
the Persian water-wheel works night and day.
"You, You," like Papiha bird is cried by me;
Ram, when will You come, so You I can see?

The tears of people who are wicked appear
like the good people who shed many a tear:
when tears of blood are streaming from eyes
then know in that heart Love certainly lies.

Disciple was burnt by fire the Guru started;
that one was burnt in fire separation fed:
that bundle that was a piece of grass today
was saved when it embraced the pile of hay.

The fire was lit and the water was aflame,
the gigantic blaze leapt from where it came:
the river that had run now remained still,
no water flowed for the fish to have its fill.

Kabir, river caught fire, blaze rose higher,
everything turned to ashes, because of fire.
If it wasn't for the fortunate help of Gopal,
the jewel beyond value would vanish as well.

The crimson cloud pressed upon the terrain,
hot fiery coals everywhere began to rain:
Kabir says that such a great fire did grow
that all the world was scorched in one blow.

On the ocean the great fire raged unchecked
and to burning cinders the river was changed:
when he woke up Kabir looked and did see
that the fish had climbed up onto the tree.

That arrow which yesterday You fired at me
has now become something I treasure dearly:
with arrow You shot yesterday hit me today,
as I can't find Truth unless it comes my way.

Kabir, what are you doing, always sleeping?
Wake and get up and your fate be lamenting.
That one lying in the grave that is silent,
can he happily sleep when his life is spent?

Kabir, what are you doing always sleeping?
Please wake and the great Lord be adoring!
You'll be made to fall asleep in another way
then your legs will be stretched out all day.

Call out, keep calling for God Who is great,
and refuse to make endless sleep your fate:
if you loudly cry your woes, night and day,
in the end He will certainly listen your way.

Kabir, it isn't an easy thing for one to do,
to call upon Name of Great God to help you;
when one juggles above the stake the cost
is that if one slips and falls then he's lost.

True love of God is praise of Name of Hari,
nothing but endless agony is all else to see!
In soul, deed and word to worship like this
is essence of all prayer, Kabir's saying is.

If the mind of the devotee is preoccupied,
with the rope of God's Name let it be tied:
for any thought in which Ram's Name is not,
is really Kali's noose, tied by a deadly knot.

Any who do not know tenderness and love,
whose tongue away from Ram's Name rove,
the birth in the world of such ones as these
is useless: their damnation will never cease.

Through his previous mistakes and evil ways
man picked up poison that on his head stays
but millions of actions are annihilated
instantly, if God he trusts and is protected.

Instantly millions of actions are wiped out
by calling on the Name; that, don't doubt:
good deeds that for ages have accumulated
will lead nowhere, unless Name's invoked.

Kabir, the essence can be found in Prayer,
and a snare is everything else that's there
in the world, which I've searched end to end:
all else is Death, unless that Name's invoked.

Kabir, what are you doing, always sleeping?
Why don't you stand up and begin searching?
The One from Whom you are now so far away
become united with again, so Kabir does say.

Kabir, what're you doing, sleeping life away?
You're surely lost if you sleep night and day.
Even Brahma himself will lose his balance,
on hearing Death's roar he'll lose his stance.

The God that the man has desired to obtain
is the God that he will obtain: that's plain.
Great thirst is not quenched by drop of dew
unless water is carried all the way through.

That one who does abandon Ram the Beloved,
and goes off to pray to another, unapproved
can be likened to the son of a prostitute.
Who's called 'Father' by one of disrepute?

When inside the mind of man Maya is staying
then let that man by Ram it be replacing:
then through vault of the sky he'll fly free,
and he will reach that City of Immortality.

Kabir, when the mind was sparked off again
fire was all over, so difficult to constrain.
Take hold of the bucket of Prayer, quickly
rush and douse fire that burns so fiercely.

Man didn't question the One Who did know,
so off he went like fools who stupidity sow.
If the blind meet only those who are blind
then who'll help them the true road to find?

Kabir, I keep saying over and over and over,
so that everyone can hear and then discover
if one calls upon Ram then that one's saved;
if that one doesn't, then he's always grieved.

Kabir says, I've told them again and again
and Brahma and Shiva also made it plain:
the Name of Ram is the Essence of Reality;
this is the teaching I give, let all hear me!

Kabir, the fragrance of the Sandalwood tree
permeates trees growing in jungle uselessly:
it has changed all that was in its vicinity,
and into something like itself, undoubtedly.

The holiness of the Saint is retained by him
in the middle of all those who commit sin,
like Sandalwood tree that cool does remain
even in poisonous snake's embrace, a chain.

Many horses and line of elephants marching,
canopies with royal insignia, flags fluttering:
being beggar is better than such prosperity,
if beggar spends days calling Ram constantly.

That great city is constructed so splendidly
and everywhere it is full of delight to see:
but if in that city no lover of Ram resides
to me that place is a desert, Kabir confides.

Kabir says, I have two companions with me,
Ram is one and the other's the Saint to see:
one of them brings to me eternal salvation,
other makes me take the Name as invocation.

A blazing fire is ambition and one who
doesn't seek power is free from worry: true.
Anyone who for power doesn't have ambition
see even Indra in the beggar's condition.

Kabir's become like a flower called Ketaki,
and all those devotees are each like a bee:
where the love of God that Kabir has blooms
there is home of Ram, there are his rooms.

Kabir, true nobility is in that family found
where one is whose love for Hari's profound:
that family where there's no lover of Hari
is like tree that grows in jungle uselessly.

Many horses and elephants, a great number;
and for a wife a king's beautiful daughter:
compare her to that water-carrying woman,
that wife of Hari's devotee, one never can.

Why talk with disrespect of the queen-to-be
and praise a woman carrying water, highly?
One dresses herself in finery for her husband
and the other prays to Ram. You understand?

Those whose understanding counts as nothing
can have undisturbed sleep when sleeping;
but when out from my ignorance I did wake,
great was the problem that I did undertake.

To that one who even while he is dreaming
the great Name of Ram keeps on whispering,
of my own skin the sincere offering I make:
to be soles of his feet, my skin off I'd take.

Oh Kabir, to Kaaba I was journeying one day
when suddenly God stood, blocking my way;
the Lord then put following question to me:
"Who was it told you Kaaba to go and see?"

Kabir, one who the Name of Ram has known
his body becomes so thin that visible's bone;
the eyes of that one, sleep does not attain,
the limbs of that one strength don't regain.

One who longs for Ram is already suffering:
let no one cause him anything distressing!
From even a single touch that one may die,
so profound is his despair so deep his sigh.

A closet or a room is not filled with rubies
and the Hamsa bird in a line never flies;
you'll not find lions hunting in big groups
and Saints never walk together in troops.

Kabir, that day is truly a very blessed day
when those Saints happen to come your way!
Take them closely into your embrace and all
of your sins away from you will then fall.

You should not be measuring their holiness
by sweetness of the words they may express:
they'll show bottom to give assurance to you
then out into the deep they will take you.

Digging and manuring is suffered by earth
and tree feels the axe cut into its girth:
the Saint tolerates words wicked and hurtful
which no others can, as they're so harmful.

Kabir, the one who makes God feel pleased
from long way off can easily be recognised:
his limbs thin and his mind dwells within,
he wanders the world unconcerned by its din.

A death neverending is life of the devotee,
living like a lord is the man of stupidity:
the stupid man cannot tell right from wrong,
his aim is to fill his belly all day long.

They reject the truth, knowing what they do
and become fascinated by all that's untrue:
Lord Ram, do not allow me any association,
even dreaming, with them: my invocation!

Oh Kabir, the Ocean's waves continue to roll
and roll in and out in this gigantic bowl!
To God's devotee I give myself as sacrifice:
to he who diving now, again in Ocean lies.

Those five bullock senses lost their way
and towards a barren field they did stray:
I offer to sacrifice myself to lover of Hari
who caught, kept them in one place, sensibly.

God's lover is like a cloth that's priceless,
yet devotee can't be soiled, become a mess;
but goddess of senses idolator's a black rag:
used whenever one wants it is its price tag.

My Lord in all forms that exist is living,
there is no seat where He is not sitting:
yet, true married bliss is for that one
in whom He is shining as the Glorious Sun.

Kabir, the Creator is staying awake forever,
there's no other who's always awake: never!
Man of senses stays awake to drink poison;
to praise God stays awake a devoted person.

Small piece of sandalwood's more worthwhile
than forest of thorny Babul heaped in a pile.
So much better is the Saint's old mud hut
than follower of goddess of senses rich rut.

Kabir, that woman's fortunate, most blessed,
who a son who is most saintly has birthed:
praising Ram he is kept far away from fear;
world would be without a son if not for her.

Though high caste, reject he who worships
goddess of senses; stay with he whose lips
praise God, even if low caste. Run from afar
to him as though he were the Lord Krishna.

Understand that it is because of selfishness
that everyone their relationship does express:
if love they feel for you has no motive
then know that such love is God's love.

Such a one it's difficult for us to discover
who will burn down his own house, no never;
who five fellows, senses, down has knocked,
and in Ram that one's always being absorbed.

Such a One it's difficult for us to discover
in Whom we are able to take refuge forever,
for the world I've seen burning as it turns
and each one in his own flame quickly burns.

Such a one it's difficult for us to discover
who will tell Secrets like the true Teacher,
and drag us out by hair in an eye's blink
as we into the ocean of existence do sink.

Such a one it's difficult for us to discover
who will recognize our existence, and favour
show to us, and then will take us as his own
to allow us to cross to open valley's zone.

That man I found it difficult to discover
who was truly a friend of Lord Ram's lover,
to whom like deer I'd give body and soul,
that due to hunter's song hasn't control.

It's very difficult to find one's location
who'll guide us all of the way to salvation,
who stays absorbed in the Eternal Bond,
who lives in the cave of the Infinite Beyond.

World quickly passes away before our eyes,
we pass before world's eyes as time flies:
such a one it's difficult for us to discover,
to hold on to our arm and save us forever.

There is never a scarcity of brave soldiers
but there is never one who a wound bears,
when the wounded is met by the wounded
the love of Ram is then greatly strengthened.

Looking for a one who loves I always wander
but I cannot find one who is a true lover:
and whenever the lover the lover does meet,
then poison is changed into nectar so sweet.

If you give milk to a snake to be drinking,
the milk into poison will also be turning:
such a one it is difficult to find and know,
who the snake and also poison will swallow.

There's not anything left that's mine in me,
all that there is is only Yours absolutely:
it's already Yours, whatever I offer to You.
Can what I give You be mine? Is it true?

That one is lost who doesn't have a Master;
that one doesn't have that One as Supporter:
so let man be of real service in every way
and then, whatever happens, come what may!

Oh Kabir, all of the world I have searched
but I didn't find anyone who is as wicked:
Kabir's worse than anyone who does exist,
there's none worse than Kabir; this, I insist.

Kabir, the Creator is perfect in every way,
no fault has He, no matter what you say:
if, in my heart I look with an open mind
all faults lie in myself, I do always find.

Since mother happened to give birth to me
I have never known one time spent happily:
from branch to another branch I've passed
and from each leaf only sorrow I've gained.

The chance went and this body isn't lasting,
and in a foreign land the Husband's staying:
Lord, please take away this shame I bear
and take away my sins and my deep despair.

If in the same way as my soul clings to You
Your Soul should happen to cling to me too,
like iron that on an anvil grows hot and red
the split that is between us would be fused.

Love and also faith in my soul do not exist,
body knows not how to behave as You insist:
with You, my Husband in this Game of Love
I don't know how to play, or how to move.

Kabir, due to stupidity I spoilt everything;
but all this to your heart don't be taking!
That which the Master hates most is pride,
it matters not if slave blunders far and wide.

Modesty, humility are possessed by the poor,
arrogance comes from the proud one's door:
full of poison is the heart of the proud one;
heart of the humble is full of Ram, the One.

This wretched one, Kabir, is imploring You
for release from this ocean of existence too:
angel of death's violent towards Your slave,
Lord, send him away and Your servant save.

That which a box made of brass can contain
cannot possibly be the Lord; I will explain:
that which permeates the whole of creation
you should call the Lord, without hesitation.

Kabir, that One as my Companion I've taken
who all the pleasure and pain has forsaken:
with Him closely united I will happily play,
and away from separation I'll always stay.

The wife forgot her Husband when led astray
and often her true Husband she did betray;
but Perfect Master woke her to her mistake
and her back to her first Husband did take.

The great Lord Himself lives inside the body:
most people don't understand this mystery;
it's like musk-deer that's always wandering,
for musk it searches grass, always sniffing.

Don't speak about that One Who's mysterious
for not to reveal His mystery is judicious:
Him, the Vedas and the Koran cannot contain
so who'd believe you if you tried explain?

What would I say if the Beloved I did see?
If I spoke of Him, no one would believe me!
God's like God, Him one can't be comparing:
it's best to joyfully praise Him with singing.

That One Who from Creation remains apart
yet holds on to Creation in His loving heart,
such a great One's only worshipped by Kabir
and others won't be worshipped by him. Hear.

Inside the blade of grass, it is my opinion,
is hiding Ram Who is the Great Mountain:
when man finds Master he experiences Hari
and he discovers Him, within his own body.

I've done nothing and still I can do nothing,
this body is not capable of doing anything:
it is God Who does whatever action 'I do',
and it's God Who made me, Kabir, 'great' too.

Kabir, what helpful actions can you now do
if Ram doesn't come here and then help you?
For every branch that you step on is unsound
and they break and fall towards the ground.

It's true that you don't do anything at all;
what has been done, 'mine' you cannot call:
if of any action you'd been the perpetrator,
there would obviously be another Creator.

How can one describe One indescribable?
To do this, I have discovered is impossible!
No matter how often Him I tried to describe
I've found it impossible Him to circumscribe.

My friend, you look here and you look there
but Kabir has now gone, disappeared forever:
into that Great Ocean the drop has merged,
so how then can it possibly be discovered?

That one who has no one, he has You, You;
that one who has You, he has all, it's true!
Great Lord, in your court full of compassion
none is allowed to commit acts of oppression.

Lord, without You, You know so very well
that I'm not worth a worthless cowrie shell:
but if You Who are so Wealthy are with me
then I'd be worth tens of thousands, easily.

One gets nothing, though standing expecting;
another is abandoned, though still waiting:
all-powerful is my Lord, some He forsakes,
some to take His gifts from sleep He wakes.

To great Ram this question is put by Kabir:
"Of the whole wide world You are Master,
You've created all and yet detached stay:
explain how this is possible, please say!"

Kabir, I had gone out to beg and then I
met the One whose generosity does never die:
to His house He did bring this beggar, me,
then I received a Treasure, a great Bounty.

Without beginning, without end, or middle,
for ever that One stays totally indivisible:
do not allow any devotee ever to be leaving
presence of Creator: this, Kabir is advising.

Kabir, besides that One Who is the Creator,
I haven't anyone else who is my benefactor:
He chooses not rich or poor, both He'll bless
while the world wraps itself in selfishness.

The great radiance of the One Supreme Being
is beyond the imagination, Kabir is saying:
it's truly impossible to describe His beauty,
the only proof of it is when it we do see.

It was good that the hail fell on the ground
for it lost itself but a new Self it found:
it changed into water after it had melted
and all the way down to the pond it flowed.

The bird flies to the soul all the way,
while in a strange land its body does stay:
there, without a beak the bird is drinking
and this country this bird is now forgetting.

Love brightly lit up the cage of the body,
an eternal flame did rise quite suddenly;
joy did wake up and all doubt then vanished
when I did meet my Spouse, the only Beloved.

All the water had turned into ice and then
the ice itself completely melted away when
all that was, then became He Who always Is:
what else is left to say, when all is His?

Joy was born when I discovered the True One
and my heart's river flooded, away did run,
all of my sins were very easily swept away
when Presence of my Lord came here to stay.

Kabir has seen the One Who is inaccessible,
Whose great glory to describe is impossible:
that Spouse, Philosopher's stone, bright Being
in my eyes was enclosed, for inner seeing.

Oh Kabir, the great radiance of the Infinite
is like countless rising suns' bright light:
being close to her Spouse the wife awakened
and the great Wonder she then contemplated.

Kabir, like a busy bee has become the Mind,
and its eternal dwelling it did then find:
that lotus which without water does bloom,
only the servants of God can see its form.

Although there is not shell nor the ocean,
and not a drop of the Pearl-producing rain:
yet that Pearl is born in body's fortress
whose summit is the absolute Nothingness.

The Inaccessible was found within the body,
a path to the Inaccessible was found by me:
Kabir says, the Experience with me did stay,
when the Perfect Master showed me the way.

Crossing boundary I entered the Boundless,
I then made my dwelling in the Nothingness:
in Palace which ascetics are not reaching,
there I've made my abode, there I'm staying.

Please look, see what's happened to Kabir,
his fate became so fortunate; listen, hear:
the One Whose mansion ascetics can't reach,
that One's now my Friend; this is my speech.

When this false creation was as yet to be,
when highway and market one couldn't see,
then the servant of Ram, Kabir, already was
taking a look over that inaccessible Pass.

I gained peace by my association with Hari,
suffering and ignorance vanished from me,
an Ocean of Bliss I enjoyed night and day
when inside my true Self manifested, to stay.

The mind is now at peace inside the body,
it no longer is outside, seeking frantically:
into still water the flame has been changed
and fire that scorches hasn't been quenched.

I discovered Reality, and I forgot the body,
when during meditation mind became steady:
I found peace, of suffering I became devoid,
when I bathed in that Nothingness, that Void.

Kabir, when my mind was firmly centered,
as reward the All-powerful Lord I obtained:
while in the ocean I spent my time searching
into my hand the Divine Diamond was falling.

When delving inside, mind found the River;
then it washed and scrubbed itself cleaner:
one searches for the depth without success,
for You are Mercy that is deep, boundless.

Thunder in the sky and ambrosia flows down,
the lotus and plantain tree are in bloom:
Kabir pays his homage to that inner place,
as is done by the few lovers of His Grace.

Kabir, when Sound of Revelation enters body
the lute resounds without strings to see:
the body, inside and out, it is pervading;
gone are thoughts and need to be wandering.

Kabir, difficult is that Path, so difficult,
and no one can discover its final result:
those who did traverse it never returned,
never returned to explain how they fared.

On top of the Path is the house of Kabir,
where Path is most slippery; listen, hear:
where even the ant can't keep its footing,
with loaded bullocks people keep travelling.

Not a one has ever come back from there
whom I could run to and ask of the danger:
and yet all of them set off on the pathway
carrying a heavy load, burdened on the way.

In that Forest where not a lion is roaming,
where not a bird through the air is flying,
where neither day nor night exists there,
Kabir is dwelling, merged in the One Forever.

All keep on saying: "Let us go, let us go!"
But I still doubt, but something I know:
they do not know the Lord, not in any way,
so where will they find safe place to stay?

The name of that Village we do not know:
if we do not know it then how can we go?
While walking along a whole age flew away,
while walking to that Village that's nearby.

Where even the ant cannot climb, and where
even the mustard seed hasn't room there,
and where neither mind nor breath can go
there I have finally reached; yes, this is so!

Kabir, that Path's an extremely difficult way
even ascetics were exhausted, couldn't stay:
but Kabir has been able to climb along it by
holding on to one who on Master does rely.

Gods, men and ascetics couldn't reach there,
and there no one at all could pass either;
it has been the greatest fortune of Kabir
to have built his hut there: listen, hear!

Breath has gone from the body and it's said
by everyone there: "That person is dead!"
Such a state when one's still alive but dies,
is so subtle that it no one can recognize.

Mystery of the Creator is impossible to know
so it's best that your intuition you follow:
if you step forward carefully, one a time,
you will eventually reach that Proof Sublime.

There's not one of them who does understand
what this country is, on which they did land:
they cannot discover that Path that is true,
because they're lost, not knowing what to do.

As I roam about I ask all the same thing,
but no one can tell one how to keep living:
as long as there's no love in heart for Hari,
how is it possible to achieve immortality?

Oh Kabir, this world does not give happiness
to one who having many friends does express:
all of those who have hearts that are bound
to the One, continuing joy in them is found.

That soul that's always trying hard to cling
to the One, that soul its release's obtaining:
he who at the same time two trumpets blows
such a hypocrite deserves blows and woes.

If a wife who is said belongs to her husband
keeps company, that is, holds another's hand:
if in her heart she should then love another
can her true Lord's grace be found by her?

I'm always thinking only of you, but you,
you're always thinking of something else too:
Kabir says, how's it possible for this to be:
one soul's in different places? A possibility?

All of the love I have is given only to You,
oh Husband Who's perfect and Who is true!
If with a smile I should talk to some other,
then let me with soot my teeth cover.

I'm slave of that One Who is full of Power,
for Whom it's not possible to have a failure:
if the faithful wife went naked in a street
wouldn't shame fall at her husband's feet?

Kabir, the shell that lies deep in the sea
cries out full of pain because it is thirsty;
it believes the whole ocean's worth nothing:
for raindrop that becomes Pearl it is longing.

Kabir, if that One you have never known,
what's the use of all knowledge ever shown?
All and everyone are born from that One,
that One isn't born from all and everyone.

Kabir, if you have knowledge of the One
then you have all knowledge under the sun;
but the one who the One has never known,
all of his knowledge is ignorance overblown.

The moment that You came into my eyes
I closed them, which of me was very wise;
I did it so that I could not see any other,
and so You weren't seen my eyes I did cover.

Oh Kabir, in my hair's part I wear vermillion
but on my eyes I don't place the collyrium,
because in my eyes my Beloved always stays
and for anyone else there's no place, always.

**3 3**

Kabir, if such a wife there happens to be
who could go and betray the One knowingly,
she will never enjoy the favour of that hand
of One Who is Supreme Being, her Husband.

I've embraced all of the torments of hell
and it caused me no fear, I honestly tell:
I've no craving for paradise I can truly say,
while far away from You, Beloved, I stay.

Kabir, I drank away all the Liquor of Hari,
I kept drinking until nothing was left for me:
Once it is baked, then Potters pot of clay
never again on the wheel does it find a way.

All the magic liquids I've sampled, I swear;
and I swear that none is like Hari's Liquor:
if only a drop the body happens to hold
then whole of the body's changed to Gold!

My body which is like a gourd-pot that's dry
with pure clear water I've filled, so say I:
when I drank my thirst still wasn't quenched
and we can see that Kabir, thirsty remained.

If by seven knots his loin-cloth is fastened
because of this the Saint isn't concerned:
with the Liquor of Ram he is so intoxicated
he sees Indra as a tramp, one who is wasted.

One drunk by Ram's Liquor one can recognize
by soberness never appearing in his eyes:
he wanders like an elephant gone crazy
and all the time he's unconscious of body.

Loving the Invisible Reality, mad elephant
from concepts is free and feels no restraint:
with Ram's Liquor he is intoxicated forever,
he's soul that's liberated, beyond the ether.

**3 4**

No fodder's eaten by elephant that's crazy,
with love his soul is tormented, never free:
if at the door of Love he is tightly tethered
he will continue to throw dust over his head.

That small packet of that Divine Ambrosia
has been unfolded, is now open to exposure:
if you meet one who thinks the way you do,
then mix it and give it to him to drink too!

In the beginning the Forest is burnt by fire,
then again it grows green, higher and higher:
To that Tree I give highest praise that's due
for after felling, to fruit it does continue.

That death which the world is always fearing
is a great joy for me: when will I be dying?
When will it be that I'll see the One Who
is over-abundant as is the Supreme Joy too.

A roar came from the one who threw spear
and the wounded one cried out even louder:
yet, after being hit by arrow of true Guru,
there where Kabir fell Kabir fell silent too!

You'll not be saved if you hide in a corner,
listen, you foolish soul, be a good listener!
Kabir, on open field be sure you're dying,
and there, war on your senses be waging.

It is impossible for cowardice to save you,
so be courageous, try to be persistent too!
Throw away from you the arrow of Mistake,
and to your hand the spear of Prayer take!

Kabir, enter the battlefield and don't fear,
for a brave soldier's never found in the rear:
he's that one who to his Master is faithful
and in his Presence fights, always watchful.

On each side that gallant soldier bravely
fights: fighting only one is not gallantry;
Kabir, for that bravery that can't be seen,
none will praise him for where he's been.

Oh Kabir, that one can be called a true hero
who with his mind constantly struggles; so
knocking those foot-soldiers the five senses,
that which's called Duality he then dispenses.

All my hesitation fled away from me when
I fell deeply in love with Hari, and then
I did challenge both lust and anger to fight
upon the field of battle, open to the Light.

The brave soldier is he who deserves praise,
who from love for his Master fights, always:
he would much prefer to be cut into pieces
than to run from the battle before it ceases.

The brave soldier doesn't flee the battlefield
between the armies he fights, doesn't yield:
any regard that he has for his death or life
he has cut from his soul with a sharp knife.

The boasting of cowards can always be heard.
Are boasts of the brave heard? Not a word!
It's only through actions you can judge those
whose faces show light: by deeds one knows!

Kabir, Love's House is approached by a way
that's an impossible path; what can one say?
Cut your head off, it under the feet trample
if Love's flavour is taste you wish to sample.


I became my true weight by cutting off head
and bought a full serve with my life. Said
Kabir: whoever wants to take, let him do so
for this is Love's price I set: head must go!

When his head a brave warrior does sever,
all hope he has for life he gives up forever,
then great God is happy and He then joyfully
meets His servant without hesitation, quickly.

It's very difficult to obtain the Love of Ram:
cowards fail, only the brave know its charm.
With your hands cut away your own head,
then Ram's Name call on; this, Kabir said.

Love of Ram is difficult for one to obtain,
it's like sword's edge that many seek in vain:
all who happen to hesitate are cut away
but all who are resolute pass over, and stay.

When for sale the great Diamond was offered
a price that was beyond belief it fetched:
flesh and the bones must both be dissolved,
to gain this bargain price of life's involved.

If I lose, well then I will be like God; so
then if I win, well then I'll win the throw:
when I am playing with the Supreme Being,
what do I care if it's my life I'm losing!

While I am remembering God's perfections,
many arrows pierce me from all directions:
although hit many times I don't run away,
to endure pain that ensues Kabir does stay!

There's nothing left to do now except fight,
there's no turning back, house out of sight,
to his Lord he then dedicates all his life,
and that brave soldier banishes all strife.

The drums of the sky all beat and resound,
and gongs of war are sounded on the ground
and on field brave soldier roars like a tiger
as the moment of his death is coming closer.

Then in his hand he takes up bright spear
and puts on the ochre robe of the warrior,
he mounts Elephant of Knowledge, goes forth
for he's ready for battlefield and his death.

Go to that one who's wounded and enquire,
who day and night's awake from pain's fire:
that One will know, Who released the arrow;
and that one who it wounded will also know.

Entranced, one who's wounded wanders here
and there; doesn't look for safety anywhere:
nothing could save him from mortal strife
for wound he is carrying will take his life.

The tree's so high the fruit hangs in the sky
and birds died being unable to fly that high:
many are the wise men who've died in vain,
Fruit was Beyond though they tried again.

In the garden Love won't be found growing,
in the market Love's not there for buying:
whoever's longing for it, king or commoner,
the price is life if he wants to be purchaser.

Kabir, the great steed of Love I did mount,
Aware of my action, risks I did not count:
the sword of Wisdom I took up in my hand,
and a great blow on Death's head I did land.

You can't hold even a fraction of a moment
and yet plans for tomorrow you still invent!
All of a sudden Death will make you its prey
like hawk instantly taking partridge away.

Once a birth in human form you've obtained
if you then miss great chance you've gained
back into whirlpool of existence you'll fall
and blow on blow will greet your downfall.

Kabir, it's like one who dreams in the night
and then eyes are opened, receiving sight:
it appears that the soul great loss suffered,
yet when one wakes up nothing is changed.

There is the mirror that exists in the heart
yet the Face can't be seen or will not start
to appear: His face will begin to appear
when Duality from the heart does disappear.

Why wander giving out water that you store?
Don't you know Ocean's at everyone's door?
That one who is always desperately thirsty
will drink no matter what the price may be.

All is obtained when one attends to the One
and lost when attention to all's paid by one:
that one who waters that Root on the inside
has many fruit and flowers he can't hide.

Oh Kabir, this body is quickly passing away;
if you can, try, see if you can make it stay.
To the service of the Saint devote your days
or else you should sing great God's praise.

Kabir, don't go about full of pride, proudly
displaying the fair beauty of your fine body:
you'll have to let it go today or tomorrow,
as snake that sheds its skin must let it go!

Oh Kabir, this body is quickly passing away;
see if you can make it come back this way!
They've gone the same way, hands empty;
all of those who millionaires used to be.

Kabir, don't go about full of pride, for you
are bag of skin with bones sticking through!
Those with canopy above, fine horse below,
also into pit someone will one day throw.

Wearing bright garments that dazzle eyes
they chew betel leaves, a costly enterprise;
yet, if they don't remember Name of Hari,
in chains led off to Death's City they'll be.

Man died after the world led him astray,
he worried about his family's honour all day.
But who'll worry about honour of your family
when your body's gone for cremation finally?

For this world your religion you did let go
and yet the world won't go with you, oh no!
With the axe your own feet you cut away
with your own hands: this Kabir does say.

In the world wandering far and wide I went
with a mandolin upon my shoulder, bent;
asking all I've seen by beating the drum
I have discovered that no one has anyone!

Where there's compassion, the Way is there,
where there is greed, sin is there to share;
where anger is there, doom can be found,
where forgiveness is, there Self does abound.

Let one who is householder practise the Way
or else let him stay where ascetic does stay:
but if ascetic is bound by his worldly ties,
great is misfortune that in wait for him lies.

Kabir, I spurred my horse on across the land
with the whip I held tightly in my hand:
may I meet my Lord when the sun's setting,
for later, night will fall, I'll be regretting.

Make sure that to Ram you are bound tightly
and by trifles don't be worried, don't worry:
the beast tied at door of the butcher's shop
how long can it hope to avoid the final chop.

There is a feast of plunder of the Name
of Ram. Take, take that for which you came
for death awaits you and life will pass away
and you'll be left to cry all night and day.

The deed of tomorrow do today, do it today;
today's deed do today before life flies away
for oppoitunities will never return, oh man,
do it now and do now as much as you can.

Tomorrow and tomorrow, and onward still,
you will postpone twenty tomorrows until;
but between today and tomorrow waits death
so do it now without wasting more breath.

"I'll pray to God tomorrow," you will say;
then tomorrow comes, "tomorrow not today."
So, in the current of all the tomorrows you
lost golden chances. No excuses! Just do!

This time is mine; oh let me stay awake!
Please let me all my opportunities take.
I don't know what the next moment'll bring,
so this precious time I'll not be wasting.

Lord! Your existence dwells in bodies all,
hidden from view beyond this earthly pall
like redness that is hidden in myrtle green,
that in its outer fibres cannot be seen.

No corner exists without God, and no nook
is there where rests a pin without Him. Look.
for Ram is before, behind and on the right,
on left and everywhere Ram comes in sight.

God dwells in the body as does in the eye
the inner pupil; yet strayed mortals try
and try and try, and seek for God without
their true self! Fools, what are you about?

The musk, it dwells in the deer's abdomen,
and the deer for the musk does wander when
it senses it. Such is the state of man;
God's within: let him seek as best he can.

The oiler's bullock toils round and round,
and still stays there to the center bound;
you, who have forgotten God, will also be,
when born, if you don't worship the Deity.

All people lived and then died in poverty,
riches no one could keep for all eternity.
Whom do you call rich? He who gains, he,
that priceless treasure of the Divinity.

I've one word for you, this advice I've given
and in that, all of the philosophy of Heaven
and all of earth does lie: lift your voice
to God and let go of all the worldly joys.

A spark of fire, thin like a mustard seed,
will destroy a very large heap of weed;
and so, the smallest name of Ram does burn
a thousand loads of grief. Mortals, learn!

Even if all the earth was paper and the seas
all seven, full of ink, and all the trees
yielded countless pens, I still couldn't write
Your virtues, God; all endeavours despite.

God is a light burning without wick or oil;
all my efforts to find Him He does foil:
God doesn't wear a personality I can see:
oh for a true Guide that'll show Him to me!

I have seen God, and yet what man on earth
can believe my words? What joy and mirth!
Sing, sing, sing of Him in sweetest ecstasy,
one God, one state, although man varied be.

The fact of all of this life does truly lie
in the remembrance of God Who's Most High;
all else I did inspect from first to last,
and found them all to death advancing fast.

The Name of God is the seed of all charms,
and that one Divine root entirely disarms
all sin. He who that Divine charm does keep
will cross the sea of pain however deep.

Think of God and say His Name all day,
control mind; this, all the Holy Books say.
Why do you die, cramming books for nothing:
this jumbled trash with wisdom glimmering?

Who takes the Name of God, that one alone
will find all the Shastric mysteries unknown;
whoever doesn't take the Name goes to Hell:
then, let him mutter the Vedas ever so well.


May misery and may sorrow be most blessed,
for they do put us to the strongest test
and make us think of God. Of what use can,
without God, be the blessings of mere man?

If in the longing for God, into many a part
skin is torn, blood drops from your heart;
still stay with God. Who remembers Him not,
be cursed with all his self, and wicked rot.


The home that does not saintly beings serve,
does not remember Ram as He does deserve,
is but a gloomy burning-place for the dead;
and by witches, wizards, fiends is inhabited.

The Name of God is like a pearl. Keep well
as your own soul. that Jewel in the shell,
so that, that great Deity of all deities
may from sorrows, hardships, you release.

Remember God in the morning when you wake
and at night before sleep God's Name take;
while sitting, standing and walking, keep
God's image pictured in your spirit deep.

As flame in stone, the Lord does lie in you;
with purity of the mind you'll see Him too;
yes, you will see the Flame itself is you,
and you are a form of the great Deity too.

Seeking the brilliant diamond that fool goes,
that poor, foolish glass-examiner; he knows
not, he, that in his home is the Treasury;
how can fools like him find their Divinity?

I thought that God was from me far away,
but, in the deep inner self, God did stay;
why so? There hung the veil of sin before
my eyes, so I couldn't see Him and be sure.

He whose heart is blinded by illusion's gleam
can never catch a glimpse of God Supreme;
that blockhead will grovel in material life,
making him much too weak for inner strife.

No one remembers God when in happiness,
but all seek Him, seek Him when in distress:
if a man thinks of Him when in prosperity
he never, never, never ever will unhappy be.

When our five senses and a sixth, our mind,
the pure light eternal of the truth do find,
add last our self, and stop floodgates seven,
death dare not stop us from gaining Heaven.

Outside of your self God is not anywhere,
dig, dig inside; see: God is there, yes there!
Whoever goes near to man is near God too,
who stays "far", beware, for He is far too.

**44**

Light is within, Light is without; delight
the eye feels when it perceives all Light;
wherever I turn, right, left, below, above,
Ram manifests Himself: all Light, all Love.

The flame of Ram is in all hearts contained,
the thoughtless mind does waver unrestrained
and the flame does not come and smoke lifts
and the mind sees not God through the rifts.

For as long as vice makes its dark abode
in the human heart there's nowhere for God;
but when the Heart's filled with God's Light
then vice's company, man leaves outright.

Senses please themselves with food and lust,
devoted lover of God: fly, for fly you must.
Oh fool, the jewel, it does escape from you,
in eating, drinking, life wears you through.

Desire for life of the senses lives not there
where Ram is. Where Ram's not, lust's there;
can opposites in one place find their rest?
The lure of sense and spirit in one breast?

When in that Center stays the perfect mind,
wherever it is, Peace it will always find;
I have so thinned the fibre of this false I
that one with God most peacefully live I.

When the flower drops down on the ground,
breaks from its twig, full bloom and round,
the deepest bud does open and is not seen;
because with God alone does lay its origin.

Why do you neglect Ram? I am so surprised,
for all will pass away that you have prized:
your youth, your beauty and your property
will meet with destruction. Can you not see?

The birth of man or woman was given to you
so that you may sing the Name of God too;
why haven't you kept that fact in your mind
and why do you other occupations find?

Don't be glad when you are seeing opulence,
when you're poor don't you feel sufferance;
because in abundance there's plentiful pain;
whatever it is, it's what Fate does ordain.

Kabir, this Maya tastes like sugar sweet,
no one wants to leave her when they meet;
I thank my Guru for knowledge that's given,
or else I would perish, scorned by Heaven.

The chain of Divine Ego ties firm and fast
slim Maya with this world. Can it at last
be broken loose? No, it certainly can't be,
because God gives it to all of humanity.

There is no patience in the loveless heart,
and love that can't say 'no' will not start;
until you have a true Master that can lead
you from mental evils, you can't be freed.

In knowledge the true Guru must be complete
and his heart with purity must be replete;
a Master like this, you from sins will free
of thoughts, words and of actions. Hear me!

Praying, dissolve yourself in form of prayer;
the lips shall speak never a word, never.
Shut the gates, don't see the outward sight,
retire within, there you will see the Light.

One who with God's great Love inspired is,
can never from the chains himself release;
it does continue with him all his life long,
in death also the passion is still strong.

The cloud of great fire comes thundering on,
and it rains down so much fire all upon
the world, Wake up, Kabir, run to its aid,
and save it, save it from this dreadful raid.

He who destroys his house, it he redeems:
who keeps, loses it. Friend, strange seems
this fact, but, no, it's so definitely true:
who totally dies does feasting death subdue.

The beads in rapid fingers do solemnly roll,
tongue's in mouth, but where is the soul?
Mind wanders in all directions, all four:
that state, we do not call prayer anymore.

As the arrow aims to fly straight to target,
so must mind: a prayer to God discharge it;
the praying mind must be so concentrated,
lips or tongue don't move, nothing is stated.

Trembling lips are not in stillness bound,
the tongue not even a single syllable sound,
the thought is silent and mind in ecstasy:
that state is the Sadhu's in all sincerity.

When in the heart the song divine does ring,
why do lips need to mutter and throat sing?
The Love of Great God impassionately sticks
without slightest troubles, to such ascetics.

If you in the inmost heart, God adore, your
hair will bristle at God's voice for sure.
We call it prayer that springing from heart
has not an outward form, has never any art.

To the home of God I wandered far and wide
but couldn't reach it for I hadn't a Guide;
I travelled for long miles away, away. away,
while the home of God a metre .away, lay.

47

Where do I search for Him, and where is He?
Found by such endeavours that One can't be;
Kabir, take him that knows the real Mystery
and by his sure guidance, Him you will see.

The fact that I was seeking here and there,
for which I spent blood of hope and care,
stung deep within me, but I could not see;
did I find it? Yes, the Guru showed it to me.

Look, see the sparkling jewel of God's Name,
studded fast in your heart of excited flame,
the Light will spread Light within, without,
and so He is explained beyond all doubt.

Why vainly persist in making outward show?
Know God from inside, God from inside know
for what business with this world have we,
because our final destination is the Deity.

He who remembers with the hope of gain,
the mansion of bliss he does finally attain,
but, he who remembers with no hope at all,
is given the Eternal Bliss of God and All.

If by the worship of a stone one can see
Great God, I'll worship lord mountain Giri;
is it best we deify the stones of the mill,
so that we can grind the flour too, at will?

The human body is your constant temple pure
and Lord God's Presence in it does endure;
remember God in you, and when that's done,
why do you need to worship lifeless stone?

My Lord, He looks for shelter in every form,
form without Him to the Law doesn't conform
and great is is the glory of form from which
God's Presence to all Humanity does reach.

In one light four and sixty lamps combine,
and, add to it, the light of moons fourteen:
can there be Light? Yes, darkness will be,
if Govind's Light does not shine brightly.

His remembrance alone gives us happiness,
His remembrance alone frees us from distress
so, remember Him and remember Him alone,
and in you God unknown will make His home.

So, win God's Love and you no one will harm
for who can resist God's all-protective arm?
Although many as the stars may be your foes
none can hurt when He loves you and knows.

Who charms of remembering God does learn
and deeply studies them, to that one I turn
and say: "You've learnt the ways of prayer,
and rightly framed mind. Be free from care!"

To turn the beads, or to think in ecstasy,
or to join our soul with God, does truly lie
all in remembrance; nothing like it, oh man!
The Saints and I know it. Know if you can.

The goddess of wealth says: "I am ever new,
yet still I can't fulfil man's hopes untrue.
How many men have I seated on the throne,
and how many into despair have I thrown?"

The true wealth in Union with God lies,
and true poverty from non-union does rise;
with me, all of happiness or all of poverty
is God; with others, in the things they see.

Collect that Wealth and watch it very close,
that it for your aid always before you goes,
for no one has seen a fool with loaded back
of possessions, find his way to God's track.

I tried all things fit for my soul's remedy,
and I found none, none except the Deity;
if but only one fraction of the life Divine
comes in, self like purest gold will shine,

I leave this speech, from here I soon depart
so, listen, listen, you after my own heart!
You, the Great Name of God will redeem:
Truth repeating itself that Truth does seem.

This old Maya is a witch that is magical,
who gives to death all who in her hands fall
and that man alone is from her hands free
who goes seeking the shelter of the Deity.

Our body is a guest that's not worth a pin,
the real actor is the soul that is within;
I don't know when this form will go away:
I know not, although I think of it all day.

In speaking and in hearing, milleniums have
rolled away, away. You, mad with Maya, save
your soul, and take the Great Name of God,
for death at your pillow waits with a rod.

Death's strength reigns supreme with dread,
and prophets like Moses have been afraid;
heaven, earth and hell, everywhere you see,
death's violence does it's work incessantly.

At the approach of death-filled winter, cries
the lord of woods, complains and deeply sighs
that the twigs (his loved ones) will depart,
that he birthed with the blood of his heart.

Don't think the man is dead when he's dead;
there is a life beyond, where forever tread
forms spiritual though not human. Look, see:
the ball of food often thins mysteriously.

When the ego vanishes and the senses die,
disturbance pauses: that, death does imply;
when all the forces in the one center meet
the demon named Death, man fears to eat.

We call him king by God prosperous made,
who rides an elephant beneath golden shade,
but do you know? That poor man does dwell
in darkness and in misery, a living hell.

That wretched person the sovereign we call,
who knows nothing of great God Ram at all,
who bows down to the world and worships it
and is enthralled by love of illusion sweet.

Leaves fall from Time's destructive stroke,
the branches laugh, jeer and sneer and joke;
but "Wait" say despairing leaves, "kind mates
today we go; but for you tomorrow waits."

The light does play about in the eye freely,
and the hero knows this in its entirety;
or, the one who the saintly Guru does find,
sees the Light of God broadly shine in mind.

Do not call your emperor or your sovereign
great, but whoever prays to a form Divine;
the greatest of them all is that one who
does meet formless God in the Beyond too.

God, I don't wish for anything from Thee,
not worldly bliss, not power nor prosperity,
except for Your Name and also the company
of Saints, both night and day unendingly.

My Lord, I want neither a crown nor throne,
I want the alms of prayer from you alone;
Lord, I do not wish for anything from You
but Your thought, roaming Eternity through.

The means of knowing the way to Heaven
is only by the Perfect Master truly given;
he who finds that means and seeks the Light
will at the end meet God's beneficial sight.

The man of God from yonder comes, behold!
Run! Meet him, and in broadened arms fold;
I do not know in what form God I'll see,
except in the Saint He shows Himself to me.

The mind does in all of its objects of desire
most sweetly roll, and then it does acquire
the knowledge of all the things in ecstasy,
and then it does roll along in saintly unity.

He whose constant work is God's tale to say
and sings the song of God night and day,
whose life is in this world, thoughts above,
oh join your heart with his, in honest love.

He whose constant work is God's tale to say
and whose work lies in that, night and day,
I, Kabir, say that even ashes become sweet
at such a Master's holy, blessed, lotus feet.

But, I warn you, oh man, beware, beware
of going to the saint whose constant care
it is to eat, to drink, to sleep, to dream,
and not to think or to talk of God Supreme.

Oh pupil! Don't listen to his tale of vice,
when hearing it the vice will you entice,
and it will make you also forgetful of Hari,
this is very serious advice so listen to me!

Who loves to hear tales and songs of God
and befriends those who their path have trod
will his true    salvation doubtlessly attain:
this is my advice and its spoken not in vain.

Whoever curbs the five senses is a recluse,
to one of the five the sense of God ensues;
who doesn't curb with force the senses five,
to him the breath of God does not arrive.

Kabir, do not teach the wisdom of that One
Who wears no form to the one who's begun
to chain all his hopes to this world of form;
but who has not, him of your wisdom inform.

Call him man who lives in bounds confined,
who having passed does bear a Sadhu's mind;
but, one who far beyond these two has gone
displays his glory near great God's throne.

I passed the limit and the boundless space
I entered, I live there, such is the case
with me. Such case by deed with all will be
so try, and by self-experience God you'll see.

The one that is in this narrow space bound,
in ignorance its praises he does propound;
but he who has gone into boundless space
has never a word to speak about his place.

It is by self-experience that one can see
and not by speech and learning, great Hari;
all this is miraculous, so know Him, oh you,
and knowing, keep that Secret and be true.

The dwelling of God has no earth, stone, no,
for it is a place that has no road to go;
God is a person, and yet He is also bodiless;
this is my insight, people, that I express.

Call him by the name of Sadhu that man who
has renounced gold and renounced women too
and one who feels no awakening of desire,
whose mind fixed, always to God does aspire.

The true man of God can't master the world;
he's a man who's defeated, elbowed, hurled;
the one who is 'defeated' goes to the Lord,
and the one 'victorious' is to death restored.

To read, to write, and all our science show,
is all but too easy: no one can let that go;
to clean the heart of vice, to hold the mind
and raise to God is most difficult you'll find.

The brilliant moon sits prominently at night
among all the planets, boasting of her light,
but, when the glorious Sun awakens, see,
all planets and the moon hide shamefully.

A thousand thousand fools have passed away
who did no good but talked night and day;
with us, the words a great requiem do find,
and it is our actions that are left behind.

Tell, why do you deform you handsome face
by shaving the head and moustache of grace?
Listen, oh man! Shave clean mind within,
for there all the passions beat, full of sin.

The monkey, he wanders from tree to tree,
like the anxious mind that jumps constantly;
until it is resting on the Great Name above,
it will delight to move and move and move.

It is the mind that fattens the one within,
it's the mind that makes one lean and thin;
mind makes one cool, mind makes one fiery,
as is the mind, so you, man, will also be.

The mind makes one rich and makes one poor
and mind is very skilful, and if at the door
of God it knocks to see Him, He will be sure
to speak to it. Let the mind not this ignore.

An infinite variety of coming, going shows
you assume, but doubt on doubt still grows,
and so, you seek the man of God without,
while He is in you. Please remove the doubt.

Yes, any fool can wear the Yogi's dress;
but, he who the mind within does repress,
one who makes the Yogi of the inward mind,
he, the childlike Saint, is of the holy kind.

The mind is impure, the body shines white,
like the clever crane with oblique sight;
so much better is the black and ugly crow
that within, without, one color does show.

Bald headed· Sadhu! Why be angry with hair?
Why shave the head and sorry features wear?
And why don't you control your rebel mind?
True work in that discretion you will find.

You feed upon the world, and put on finery,
then you go about and swagger pompously;
cunning rogue, the lane where God declares
you go and pollute with your wicked wares.

Please, shave mind that lustful desires bear;
why pluck the innocent and harmless hair?
All deeds result from many mental energies:
why blame the hair? Please tell me, please.

The hairy head of sinful mind go and shave,
cut off the desires that for evil crave;
hold fast the five senses by mind controlled
and all the world shall you in honour hold.

True religion does not consist in the bead
rolled in the hand and red mark on head;
you slave of poor beads, what can you do,
when your impure minds wrong paths pursue?

Keep watchful guard: your mind watch over
with patience; don't let it leave the door;
don't entertain fear, but, doubtless, pray
to God only: this is what Kabir does say.

When once the heart thirsts for God's Love,
the mind remains ecstatic in His sweet Love.
false sights, sense perceptions fly too far;
why use words? There, God's where you are.

The unwise and the immoral don't see right;
it is they who go to church day and night;
they know that the body's the church of God
yet they seek Him in the stony-built abode.

For God's thought, let the mind be purified;
for prayer, let your heart in love be tried;
no iron turns into gold when it's parted by
something from elixir, how ever you may try.

How listlessly and also busy in her talk
the graceful water-carrying girl does walk!
Yet all of her mind is given up to the pot,
so concentrate in God your wavering thought.

How very heartily the greedy wretch adores
his gathered hoards, and every time deplores
each thought of wealth! So, fix your mind
on God; persist, and His Light you'll find.

It's such a mad unlawful thing we desire,
yet not so mad in God's Love: pure like fire
if that flame rises in our heart, we will go
to God unhampered by either friend or foe.

I lost my conscious self in deepest ecstasy
and there was no light whereby I could see,
then I saw Him. Since then, I live my life
in His true service free from mortal strife.

The Sage is a deep well that is milky sweet;
go deep in it and you will most surely meet
the flowing julep of truthful Philosophy;
drink deep from it, still much left shall be.

I saw Light of Knowledge that makes clear
all secrets, and I knew Him without fear.
God, to us, all the Vedas haven t explained;
Him I now serve, Him I have now attained.

Who dwells far beyond the Heavens bound,
is my great Lord Who was in my self found;
He wears no form, no shape, and is no line:
the formless, shapeless, lineless Form Divine.

When I was only I, then God could not be;
now only God is, and now I cannot see me;
the full Light descends in my inner heart,
and the all-pervading dark did then depart.

The Spirit dwells in that great region rare
where Heavenly music the first 'BE' cheer,
where ever is burning the light of Eternity,
where music sounds, where the soul is free.

All spirits issued from one Country fair,
all of them descended to the country here,
but, on the middle plains great sufferance
created amongst them a cursed difference.

Since when Kabir gave up, began serving God
and reached the neverperishing Divine Abode
and the subject and object then died away,
and the I and You in one form mingled lay.

The Guru helped and showed the Path to me,
and then I did lose the stock of quality
and senses; then access to God I did gain;
so why should I then philosophise in vain?

You need guidance as long as you're chained
by limits. But when once you have attained
the Limitless, you don't need it; for then,
by Self-experience you have Understanding.

The world wears a form that our eyes view;
it perishes, and so then, formless is true;
that Essence-Name, only that One lives:
only the formless, nameless Essence survives.

Why spend all your life in sleep and sleep?
Wake up and pray and long, long hours keep!
one day you will your long sleep commence,
then sleep with nothing for a disturbance.

The I is I for as long as the candle burns,
wake up the I until light returns, returns;
when the oil is less then gone is the light,
the I will sleep forever, day and night.

Oh mortal, why have you all your senses lost
and why sleep when need be cautious most?
Behold! Death stands tiptoe over your head,
a moment, then you'll fall upon your bed.

The living Self to your own self explain,
or else your birth and life will be in vain;
when born, forget not Self in joy or mirth,
or else, life will rack spindles of rebirth.

My ignorance continues to occupy my mind
though I've heard most words of every kind;
your iron-will preserves its original state
until touched by magic stone of golden trait.

Why should you know many? Know the Unity;
what good is there in knowing the diversity
if you don't know the central Force? Fun!
The One creates the all, not all the One.

Just as a certain tree with too much rain
is withered, so also man's desire so vain
is not satisfied, but it grows and grows:
one fruit of gained desire another sows!

The julep doesn't please the one of desire,
he seeks to stimulate the senses with fire;
in eating, drinking, he's worn out fully,
and also in the lap of the senses' ecstasy.

He that seeks, one...money and women...two,
finds nothing at the end but a poison true;
the strength of that poison is stronger by
their very sight; and who eats it will die!

In the unceasing chant of God's great Name
the ego ran away and then God I became;
to lay my life before Your feet I yearn,
You here You there, You everywhere I turn.

Ram and Kabir are as One in form and fate,
though tongue, ear, do give them dual state;
he who pronounces Ram and Kabir as two,
that man, beware! For he hasn't had a Guru.

The name of Kabir shines quick and bright
like star eternal in this Kaliyuga's night;
the robe of service to the Lord I do wear,
I leave my name for all who live in prayer.

Kabir is God's pet dog who is named Moti,
he has Love's chain around his neck tightly;
pull this way or that way and he will go,
so then he does as God wants him to do.

To serve is hard, so hard it is to serve,
but I do serve the servants. So I deserve
not even that. To me that life is complete
that falls as thin straw crushed by feet.

I go up onto the topmost hill to loudly cry,
I cry from there, to all of humanity I cry;
listen! Oh mortals! Death waits at the door.
You who have ears to hear I speak no more.

All perish, perish in the snare of death,
all perish: all who breathe the vital breath;
but, who God's constant slave does remain,
escapes from death and doesn't live in vain.

The world sunk in deep sorrows does lament,
because one drop of life is vainly spent;
but, who does think: so many drops are lost
that the **whole** cycle is complete, almost.

The birth of being a man was given to you
to pray to God and think of **great** God true;
why do you bind yourself in **your own** snare?
To do all the tasks alloted, do you care?

Blessed is man's life with fortune's hand:
it is not frequent. Don't waste it, friend!
A fruit **that** is once dropped by mother tree
cannot cling back to it. Now, can you see?

Control the inward struggle of your heart
and strife and lack of peace will depart;
give up things that bear the stamp of Fall,
catch onto the Path of life, life Eternal.

I have destroyed my house, burnt it entire,
and so, conquered death and sorrow's fire;
if you too, wish, then come along with me,
give up your home, win peace, and be free.

Things seeming real will perish soon or late,
whatever has a name fixed also has a date;
Kabir, then hold to the secret Essence given
by your Guru, to lift you to Highest Heaven.

Whoever has been born, is also born to die,
may he be king or be a wretch in poverty;
one will ascend in pomp to the royal throne,
one lives bound in chains: so all have gone.

This iron age soon takes the life of a man,
so then, think of Him as often as you can
in this short span, for possible it is not
to call Him while in meditative thought.

What dies is man's lower self called life,
the spirit is all free from deadly strife,
all free from birth and death, it lives there
where God lives in Heaven's perfect care.

When I and God are One, if God does die
then dies this Ego merged in God, this I;
but, if the Thou...God...never does perish,
how can you say that I'm assigned to death?

If you think conquest of this world is vain,
then finally Peace sublime you will attain;
destroy the house where inside passions live;
burn it, be free: then in Peace you'll live.

I'll never turn my beads in solemn prayer,
my lips don't mutter any musings, ever;
I just sit at ease with a concentrated mind,
and God finds me, Him I don't have to find.

The thought of body thins off in His Name,
the estate of self dissolves in the flame;
when higher still in prayer we do advance,
God and the Ego blend in the one Expanse.

If from your inmost heart you worship Him,
your grief will vanish and all sorrows grim;
keep faith in God, and then your prayer do,
then all the iron will become gold in you.

Reiterating the Name of God I have now lost
self-love and self-feeling, self-fear almost;
all pain of the upper senses has been dead
for I've met my God and been by Guru lead.

Oh Kabir, awaken your senses, hear, hear;
and daily think of God all round the year;
who does this will wash his sins at last,
accumulated through all of the ages past.

There is nothing of me in me, yes it's true:
whatever there's of me belongs only to You;
take back, Lord, what is Your right of claim
for what do I lose? I and You are the same.

On this earth there's nothing living of me;
I am not anything but You, can't you see?
We think and think with inner eye Divine,
and find in all the Light of God does shine.

The seeker after Truth through distant lands
does wander, crossing fields, woods, sands:
finding Him not, though in Him the Truth is;
let him have confidence, then Truth he sees.

God says this: "In every inner self I dwell,
but no one to know Me does endeavour well;
My energy does work in each and every deed
and in My audible Divine Name can be read."

Don't let mind with this world be content
because, that is completely insignificant;
roll on the beads of mind, the mind within,
and all around you the Light shall begin.

Please, what advantage in the beads does lie
that they do not relieve you of your agony;
make mind your wreath of beads, control
your mind and at God's feet place your soul.

The wreath of beads if worn in mind is best
and only sheer hypocrisy is all the rest;
now see! The Bori's shop is full of beads,
but say, who there the name of God reads?

You make rounded beads by chopping wood,
and smoothing it, then thrust a tool: good!
But, what the deuce can all these pieces do
if he who rolls them is a man who's untrue?

Wooden beads and head-mark are all show,
the current of prayer does elsewhere flow;
I, Kabir, say that who seeks You to wear
should first control five senses with care.

When the five senses are by vices supplied
they get powerfully strong and full of pride,
the mind then pampers them without control
and they all break the chariot of the soul.

If you control the mind through self-mastery
don't let it go beyond the self's boundary;
and when impelled by vice it strives to fly,
then beat that monster back revengefully.

At first my mind was also a plundering thief
and caused much damage. Then I found relief
from its distress, by tracing true purity;
and now, I wait on the compassionate Deity.

The beads in harmless fingers roll and roll,
but, how very unsteady is the inward soul?
Your feet lie fixed in Maya's mud too deep;
how can you thoughts of self-salvation keep?

Oh Kabir, the best services are these two:
one, of great God, the other of the Guru;
the Guru does the Name of Worship teach,
and God does give Eternal salvation to each.

A formless body God does keep in His sight,
He can be served with love to His delight;
listen, you up to that formless One give,
then you shall the title of 'Saint' receive.

The mind has many hues of many a kind,
and in it one will constant changes find;
the mind that wears one hue is almost none:
that steady mind per million is hardly one.

The mind creates defeats and also victories;
in mind, one yes, lies: other no, too lies;
but if the mind once settles on the Lord,
to its first peace it will finally be restored

At times the mind ascends to regions high,
at times to the lowest point it does fly,
at times it is from the world remote, free,
and at times it's entangled in its misery.

Two aspects of its own the Illusion wears,
whoever knows that, then him Illusion fears;
the higher aspect will join man with God,
the lower form takes him to Hell's abode.

The higher Love sits high up on the tree,
the man of God ascends and eats with glee;
the lower love sits low upon the ground,
and eats what on the filthy soil is found.

The man of God the Illusion does enthrall,
while at its feet it causes fools to fall;
the senseless fondle it, it's their favourite;
away from the sensible it takes its flight.

THIS higher Love is attracting us to God.
and THAT lower to other sex; THAT's a fraud
and THIS is true; THIS, Saint: THAT, slave;
these are the various tricks Maya does have.

The heart of man around the Illusion's light
like a moth does waver, until it falls right
into the fire. If some Master who is true
then saves us, we do the path of God pursue.

That wretched person the sovereign we call,
who doesn't know anything about Ram at all,
who bows to the world and who worships it,
is enthralled by the love of illusion sweet.

Illusion is a roguish-hearted painted shrew
that ravishes, kills whoever it does pursue;
the Self does in its own way content remain
and tells to all the others: "It's all vain."

Who with the traffic of the world does tie
his heart, doesn't do one deed successfully;
unfortunately, the man never meets his Lord,
not Maya also: but to death he is restored.

The lovers: the man and the Illusion sweet,
embrace too fast and kiss when they meet;
the foolish man doesn't see with both eyes,
and doesn't heed the vulgar in her qualities.

This wicked damsel as sweet Illusion's called
makes father and son fight, both enthralled;
with her blind love she does the boy excite
to poison the Guru with an evil sleight.

Kabir, your inner mind please do recognise
and draw a lesson that from here does rise;
if you can hold these five senses under sway
you will make pupils of all men someday.

The soap is God's Name and the washerman
is Saint, cleaning with knowledge as he can,
the sight's washing-stone where on to wash;
and God, He will appear from a steady lash.

With the soap of God's Name please clean
your unclean self and soul that is within;
cry to the Lord: Name of the Lord you cry
and from all five corners all sins will fly.

Make mind firm and stop it when it flies;
sing of Great God, sing in deepest ecstasies,
try a million ways, if need, a million more;
without peace of salvation be not so sure.

You did not at first hold it under control,
how can you now hope to reclaim the soul?
And now in the traffic of the world it lies,
beat your brain now, for it flies, it flies.

When to the mind the passions don't appeal,
the bliss of the body you gain if you will;
I, Kabir, I do say that when passions die,
man will attain to God Who is Most High.

The mind, it rules over all within our view,
and always forces us to do as it would do;
but, mind who rules whoever rules the mind:
Hail! You're a Hero of Heaven's Saintly kind.

The five senses are most unsaintly, oh man,
and the mind does over-rule them as it can,
the soul that lets reins of passion loose
is dragged into the depths of life's abuse.

I voyage out in a boat that's of paper made
and have to through the mighty Ganges wade
and round me are those companions five,
of evil! Tell me, will I sink or stay alive?

Quite worthless is all your Vedic philosophy,
and worthless is all that in scriptures be,
and the Gita too doesn't help in this side:
the helper's the Master, there's none beside.

I call that man a downright lying hypocrite,
that man who talks but does not do a bit;
that liar carries a coward's transparent face
before God, and walks with frightened pace.

What meaning do all of the speeches have?
It is Action, that to us declares the Path;
it is a fort made of shadow built in air,
...words, that do not action's garment wear.

It is like a poisonous clever thing to do;
it's not hard to speak and then off to go;
that one who does, as he also does declare,
can out of poison a julep sweet prepare.

The house is desolate, call out the name
and walls will echo nothing but the same;
do you the face of God expect to really see
in such an unenlightened, shallow society?

The bitch-dog of a Saint I do much prefer
to that one who is the evil one's mother;
the former will the pious true prayer hear,
the latter will all scandalizers only rear.

All of the ignorant ones will sit together,
scandalize or call names and gossip gather;
blessed be that pig who the village sweeps,
who all of the muddy roads so decent keeps.

Thank God that the ignorant are born here,
that scandalize those who are far and near;
they wash them clean of all their sinfulness,
and go to hell in lieu, full of distress.

There is a bright mirror in the inner heart,
from where the rays of Heaven to you dart;
brush off the selfish mind's dark duality,
and all Light will manifest for you to see.

Until the body meets with the higher mind,
it will its constant degradation always find;
it will like a black and bitter dump remain:
even if it's painted up it would be in vain.

Oh sharp intelligence, oh beware, beware,
don't waste yourself in ignorance; take care
because when you fall victim to death too,
what will the old body's empty scabbard do?

It's a paradox that the mind is like a bird
that has no wings, yet flies skies that gird
the whole universe, and in it it does contain
the soul of what it wants the most to gain.

Why do you talk of the seven oceans' gales?
Those of the mind are numberless. Wails
the man, the ship of whose soul sinks low,
caught by gales; laughs, who safely does row.

The mind is at the mercy of the thought
of passion! Hold on to it fast! Let it not
run with the current of tide and tasty vice
inside the mind. Back, what can it entice?

Oh Kabir, the mind is not only one energy,
it will become whatever it delights to be;
if it wishes, well then God it ever adores,
if not, it feeds fat on passion's stores.

Bravo, if you have given up the clever mind
and body, thrown off load of every kind;
but, don't say you have given up these all,
because then there's imminent a mighty fall.

Against yourself there's no enemy who'll rise
if your mind in quiet composure always lies;
shake off your ego that's in ignorance dark,
and all will be your friend; this, you mark!

Thin is the Way that to Heaven does lead,
like the tenth part of a tiny mustard seed;
the mind will become as bulky as a mountain
and then how will you ever enter, man?

For as long as the body does exist in life,
still will continue fear, grief and strife;
when thoughts of body Maya-mind does leave
then the gates of Heaven it will perceive.

The mind makes vice a virtue, virtue vice,
in it there lies bravery and also cowardice;
if the mind does on the vacant Center rest,
the Light of God will shine in your breast.

Dissolve the mind in that which burns in you
and let it fly free like paper kite in blue;
with that the 'I' will vanish in the space,
and your face you will see in Heaven's face.

All thoughts cease when once God sees mind,
then in itself it will its calmness find,
all actions and all duties will then cease,
when fixed on God the mind sits at ease.

Worse than black poison is a bitter speech
from where destruction's fire to many reach;
the Sadhu speaks words that're full of bliss,
from which rain forth all honeyed happiness.

The kind ones serve God in all of humanity,
but no one does try to serve God devotedly;
if you only for worldly happiness do aspire,
on you are closed ways of service higher.

We don't know what the next moment will be
and yet, think of tomorrow and its finery;
as a hawk a partridge does swiftly catch,
so you, man, this sudden death will snatch.

Kabir, why do you wander in such neglect,
why are you sleeping? Can you not detect
the fiend, death, beneath your pillow hidden
as thieves do hide in the darkness unseen.

Kabir, this day that is today, it is not
tomorrow with opportunity fearfully bought;
beware! If you are wise, beware, beware:
between the two days is that dreadful fear.

This is the moment so hold it by the lock;
if you do lose it, you will have to knock
about on a misleading road and have to bear
a thousand kicks, as clay the potter's. Hear!

None will come, your disease offer to share;
when dead, to keep you no one will dare;
then, enter into friendship with that One
Who keeps you forever when you keep none.

To take the birth of a man, to enter here,
and not to think of God in silent prayer
is like constructing a deep-bottomed well
with not even a drop of water in its cell.

One word in us real affection does create,
another starts contempt and vicious hate,
one word will sow deep the seeds of enmity,
one word the ties of friendship firmly tie.

You should speak the word of universal love
and not be proud of things that're up above;
you are your own friend and your own enemy
and all find Life in the Word of the Deity.

Give up the lower self, the 'I' that's in you
and you your word deliver forcefully too;
the men about will from you bliss derive,
and your life too shall be blessedly alive.

The Pundit bathes very early in the morn,
practices ablutions ever since being born,
and self-contented thinks he has been pure,
he sees no light with inner eye, be sure.

He bathes with clear waters that are deep
and all the holy practices he does keep,
but, still, to death the Pundit falls prey,
please, has he worshipped God a single day?


His house he builds on holy Kashi's banks
and bathes hard every day in its pure tanks;
but can he ever eternal salvation acquire?
Does he in complete devotion to God retire?

Oh Kabir, this Maya tastes like sugar sweet,
none likes her when her he does meet,
I thank you, my Guru, for knowledge given,
or else I'd have perished, scorned by Heaven.

If man leaves not self, Maya leaves him not;
let him not wrangle with her when caught,
but let him for some relief towards God look
for only God can loosen Maya from the yoke.

Kabir, this old hag Maya is a witch of fire,
that swallows the world whole and entire;
but, me she dare not swallow, never, never,
for I rely on Ram for ever and forever.

What could I tell you about this Iron Age?
In this vast sea of Maya, the fool and sage,
all, all are drowned. They've left their God
in search of the world. Isn't this a fraud?

To people, how often, often I explain,
how often, how often, but it is all in vain;
you mortals, catch this Maya-bullock's tail
to cross the stream of life? How laughable!

"The world is all show, all this is a show,"
is said by all, but not a one comes to know
the inner meaning of this illusion. What
doesn't leave its hold on the mind, is that.

"Don't give yourself to it, give up the show"
is said by all. In this way, Maya cannot go.
That one receives from her a hundreds slaps,
whoever tries to leave her alluring traps.

The fool who is unlucky thinks in his mind
that he has forsaken Maya, and he does find
his home in lonely woods. But Maya's strife
hangs on his heart; in vain he wastes life.

Who in his small self does his mind surround
and straining for it, true purity has found,
and stands in Eternal Essence of the Lord,
shall be to first Innocence totally restored.

Whoever gives up the mind, he gives up all,
the mind once given up, body too does fall;
whoever has to God his mind and body given
like me will in God's service, rise to Heaven.

Into a thin dusty powder I myself reduce,
flay off the skin and make body void of use
and cut up the tongue into a thousand parts
yet, only God's Name from it ever starts.

When do you know mind peace has attained?
When you've knowledge of Unknown gained;
the darkness then becomes visible by Light,
as if bright lamp destroys the dark of night.

The leaves while dropping on the ground say
to the lord of forests: "Oh dear lord, today
we leave, never again by chance to meet;
when will we meet, father dear and sweet?"

The lord of forests then does deeply groan:
"Listen, my children, I will follow soon
your way. The Lord has so arranged the law:
one comes, another leaves Death's claw."

The buds all complain in an uproarious tone,
when the gardener comes to work at dawn,
shouting: "Pluck off blossomed flowers today
and tomorrow our turn we will then obey!"

The wheel of Time it does roll on and on,
I see, and I cry that as the grinding stone
leaves not a corn uncrushed, so in its pride
death leaves no life behind in its fast tide.

The corn that lies there on the circle will
be crushed between two stones of the mill;
but that which sticks to the center close
won't feel crush of death's furious blows.

Ah, dear, dear friend, awake, awake, awake,
death by your pillow stands. Oh please take
yourself in the pursuit of Great God's love:
oblivion-bound, wake up, seek Divine Love.

We die and die and many aeons roll and roll
and Time doesn't die for eternal is its soul;
I, named Kabir, who's servant of the Lord,
am dead to life and won't to it be restored.

The world fears death but I don't fear death
at all: it's because I am in love with death.
When shall I die and meet my God, oh when?
To merge myself in Eternal Godhead, then?

"Death is good, we wish to die," some say;
but they have not died. I have passed away
even in life. Now nothing remains to die:
even my shadow has died. Now I'm not I.

**7 3**

All my senses are dead and dead's Maya too;
my body's dead and dead are doubts untrue.
The deathless soul is not dead. How can
then, I, Kabir, be dead? Now you say, man

We die and die and all the aeons roll away;
the wife her husband, mother, son, someday
sees that all are dead. But I Kabir am dead,
but with Ram united, plunged in the Godhead.

As we walk or we sit or as we lie prostrate
one shadow trails behind us, by us, straight,
or, sits by us or beside us does also lie;
whoever is a real hero, knows this mystery.

The Higher Self lives in that realm above
where there's no difference and all is Love;
there the Word Divine Unity does procure,
and here to the body duality does ensue.

The secret comes fom secrecy that's unknown
but, coming here it does catch a contagion;
be really zealous in pursuit of the Unknown,
and all the evils captured will have gone.

Kabir, the soul wears the cloak of caste
and varied form until it reaches its last;
the Lord is casteless, formless, sexless too,
and so, in all forms, finds His mansion due.

The Lord planned the universe and He framed
the law of governance. Before it was named
yours, oh soul, He threw His mask on you,
and vanished into the realm of Mystery too.

One seed has brought forth all parts we see,
this vast expanse is outcome of His "BE";
oh wicked man, blind and ignorant and rude,
why forget He Who is the Parent so good?

One seed brought forth all parts that are;
some name of man, some name 'woman' bear;
that fruitful seed lies rooted everywhere,
so see Him in your heart, for He is there.

Know you yourself with your efforts true,
and know Ram inhabits all forms in view;
listen, you've been bound by the unreal you,
and, so, you've now forgotten the real You.

Made of the five elements, this prison-cage
is not our own. The self rests on that stage
which cannot be attained by all senses, all,
nor can be seen, nor can it be known at all.

Ram is the only genuine Friend of the soul,
Neighbour, Father, Brother, Him we may call;
without Him all our relatives are untrue,
with selfish objectives our love they pursue.

You meet God, if this man you should meet;
the mind then stable, stands in his trust;
Saint is nothing but body of Hari, yes he is:
like the flower where the sweet perfume is!

If honour lifts your head and makes you glad
and if insult makes you angry and too sad,
you remember then that Kabir says to you
that you're gripped by Maya's passion too.

Where the tree grows without stem or seed,
where the root sprouts without soil to feed,
where the color shines with no water, there
the Root primordial of the soul does rear.

In the never ceasing chant of God's Name,
mind becomes absorbed in the Deity's flame;
when once the mind is lost in You, Divinity,
it has finally found its Goal of Eternity.

I came into this world and what've I done?
And what shall I do before away I'm gone?
Not of this world, not of that I've been;
this way I've lost my God, the true Origin.

As long as in the heart the passions reign,
those of greed, debauchery, ambitions vain,
then are both the teacher and the taught
at equal fault, differing not even a jot.

Kabir, it is known the body perishes away,
then serve, serve the Saint night and day;
oh yes, until this body your control obeys,
know Him, knower, singer sing His praise.

Ah, you idiot, why do you your body swell?
Why do you pamper your body? Can you tell?
Weak fool, you don't know beneath what tree
your fattened bones will forever buried be.


If it is not today, if it is not tomorrow, hey
then a little later in the woods it'll stay,
and men will tread over your grave unknown
and cattle'll graze grass that on it's grown.

Name you knew not, as long as is breath,
you did not settle alone on Ram until death;
you were like a stone born to mother's fate:
in vain the woman bore nine months' weight.


A thousand spites be on that life lived low,
that prays not to God, nor to love, and so,
it passes on, this life like smoke away,
away does vanish. Oh mortals, live to pray.

This self is but a form fine-framed of clay,
whose name's man. He comes, then goes away
then comes, goes, and so spins on the rack,
with a small space each time he comes back.

This particle of dust, it does laugh and say:
"What fun, for many a potter passed away
since I was shaped. Even mighty sovereigns
have gone away like Ravan, Lanka's prince."

The bellows blow out when the light is out,
how can the hammer beat the smith without?
When once the light of life ceases to burn,
to what advantage then does the body turn?

Death is our constant friend. Man is to die.
Why does he nurse the hope of body? Why?
Then, worship God for these days you exist
in this cage; and then parting don't resist.

We don't know what the next moment will be
but, we think of tomorrow and its finery;
as like a hawk a partridge swift does catch,
so you man, this sudden death will snatch.

All of the earth is pure like godly Banaras,
and all water is sacred, like the Ganges is;
so keep pure your inner self, because purity
is knowledge; who knows this is the Deity.

Forget your self and God will come to you,
when God descends, what else can ensue?
Such is Ram's story and most is unspeakable:
you think when self's lost He comes to you?


When all worldly thoughts vacate the mind,
there, you Kabir, Great God alone shall find;
he who has seen the Lord with naked eye
pervades the earth, the ocean, and the sky.

If the ego should vanish in that ecstasy
of Love, God's one with the blessed devotee;
how can the Lord in a home be satisfied,
where in that ego dwells a state of pride?

You may have discarded your outward pride,
but, have you flung the inner pride aside?
Through pride you don't listen to the Sage,
and do not rise to highest Heaven's stage.

In worldly traffic you passed all your life:
you writhed and wrangled in worldly strife;
you passed away, world didn't go with you,
fool, and all of this you did knowingly, too.

Give away this sham which we Illusion call,
and pray to God. All this is vain, all, all;
the birth of a man and its great joy do not
return too often upon the wheel of his lot.

The Illusion is a wicked wench that makes
her devotee have no faith in God and takes
his zeal away from Him. Black-faced fiend,
doesn't let lip say "Ram"; such an evil mind.

I seek to meet my God with a heart of fire,
in Hope's sweet madness high I do aspire,
and yet this sweet demon comes in the way
and weans me from God with a coyness gay.

If a man leaves not Maya, it leaves him not;
don't let him wrangle with it when caught;
but, let him for relief towards God look,
for, He alone will loosen us from the yoke.

Don't give your alms to that one in charity
who men call Brahman, but rogue may be;
this fellow goes with all possessed to hell
taking with him the layman, blind as well.

Let any one practise all of the practices,
let him roll beads on that do never cease;
but as long as that one God remembers not,
all Divine blessings are beyond all thought.

The fish that in water of the Ganges dwell,
despite a thousand washes still badly smell;
not by washing outside will the inner dirt go
and the body will not name God! Oh no, no!

Kabir, the bookworm Pundit's high-flying tale
is like a boat that a scoundrel does sail,
and in it the blind and simple fools do sit
listening, but he who leads knows not a bit.

The fellow learns and tells what he learns
about the soul, yet in pursuit of ego yearns;
the Pundit doubts the All, knows not the I:
behold that teacher who is full of vanity.

My mind remembers Ram, thinks of Ram alone
and in Ram grows as it never has grown;
when the mind has become a second Deity,
who then shall I bow down to in humility?

All speak their words and sentences and all,
but from no lips the secret Word does fall;
that Word the human tongue pronounces not;
that Word is to be known alone in thought.

In search of that Word many lost their lives
and many lost their crowns. He who arrives
at the right end of the Word, giving forth,
that one inherits the Kingdom beyond earth.

My Word the Light of Truth does indicate;
don't leave my Word where Truth's incarnate.
If you eternal redemption desire to obtain,
then, know that Word and say it not in vain.

Name of God from his tongue escapes not,
and evil reigns supreme in all his thought;
he doesn't know the truth that in him lies,
and all of his false wisdom he speechifies.

A thousand long tales let the Pundit narrate
what use if he doesn't know soul's state;
as long as the Sun doesn't wake with light,
still reigns supreme the darkness of night.

The mind is tired of all of its joys, and now
it sits at ease. How can it say more, how?
It centers now upon that one Word unknown,
with a million looks, with secrecy hard won.

Like Illusion (Maya), there is no such chief
in love or beauty, and like mind no thief;
none knows this except for the man of God,
who else pretends, believe me, is a fraud.

The Knowers meet their Heaven in one way;
the not-Knowers always another law obey;
the Knowers who've caught the Divine Light
in every corner meet His glorious sight.

Don't go after that sage hungering for books
who reads them to people with grave looks;
go to the Knower of all the mysteries,
then that will end all of life's anxieties.

To itself the magnet attracts the steel;
so, men of wisdom Kabir's Word will feel;
my Word will relieve you, you son of man,
from monster death. Hear me! Surely you can.

He is in all his cleverness a bright popinjay,
but wears his life in a cage night and day;
his true existence the fellow does not know,
and claims grave problems to explain! Woe!

Let all of his wisdom to the hearth retire;
cast his knowledge of monster death in fire!
That hypocrite knowing not love nor prayer
Lord, burn off his soul in care and fear.

Talk language sweet with whom you converse
that will true happiness in others nurse;
sweet words are a means the heart to win,
leave off bitter words; from them abstain.

With patience bear the insult of your foe,
and feel content; pride meets requited woe;
Amrish the great monarch his hands did fold
before Durvas. What rank does he now hold?

What property of ours is stolen by the crow!
What mass of wealth a cuckoo does bestow!
Yet one we love and the other we do hate,
for sweet words in us love does consecrate.

In a mere perusal the world has perished,
but I'm afraid that none have been Learned;
he can be Learned who this word does know:
Love: whose letters spell both joy and woe.

I thought I could by study, Paradise attain;
believe me all my study was all in vain;
I took myself to Bhakti Yoga practice, then,
and met God, now I'm called mad by men.

One word is full of juicy, joyful happiness,
another is laden with heart-burnt distress;
one word will bind the victim in the snare
and another will release him from all care.

Difference exists between speech and speech
so to the inner Word let your ear reach;
hold that Word that Path of God declares:
in light hopes and lightness, dark despairs.

Whoever over his tongue holds firm control,
the Universe is subdued by his Master-Soul.
Listen to what the great Saints have to say:
bad speech sows the seeds of constant fray.

Lips don't tremble and tongue doesn't shake,
throat doesn't say Name when it you take;
the knowledge of that mysterious speech
the uncommon Sadhus too only rarely reach.

The path of that Word you shall also realize
by listening to the Master's teaching wise;
without that hidden Word nothing is yours,
so, see, and you'll find that the light pours.

Kabir, this Illusion is an old prostitute;
she squeezes out all that's in her pursuit;
no one does ever enjoy her bliss entirely,
we take and wish for still more, indefinitely.

Do not pursue Maya, Maya do not pursue,
throw Maya aside, your love for her subdue;
great sages like Narad become her prey,
what hope to save you then, oh mortal say.

Who speaks one way but acts another way
is not a man, but a dog that does still bay;
his words are vacant; dog's death he'll die,
repeated over and over in death's misery.

You your word and still your word speak,
though your word is lifeless, don't be weak;
one word will give you balm sweet and sound
and another will cause an injurious wound.

In You and You, all You only does appear,
thinking of You the mind in You lives here;
when once the mind dissolves in You and You
it's reached the Goal that's Eternally True.

When all the lower passions do die away,
you're in love with the Guru you could say;
when affected neither by joy nor by misery,
you are then immersed in the true Divinity.

82

The false Guru who does whisper in the ear
creates a kind of gold of hope and fear;
On Who to the boundless Space does lead,
oh hear, that is the true Guru we all need.

Your false Guru is like the greedy animal,
his pupil's a tempted beast who's too dull
to teach and learn. So see the rotten game:
their boat of mud, it perishes all the same.

That false Guru, he yearns for unjust wealth
and a pupil who has no faith in himself;
throw both of these rotten devils in a well
that has no water, like that of deepest Hell.

Oh stupid mortals, do not call him the Guru
who is entangled in this world that's untrue.
Why call Guru who you the Path can't show,
who seeks pleasure, Knowledge doesn't know.

Do not call upon the imaginary goddesses,
or painted gods of sun and moon that cease
to be true. The true Saint and God alone
are great, and live with us when all is gone.

If with man God is displeased, there's still
one Source to show the Path...the Guru will;
but, if with us the Guru becomes displeased,
by nothing would God's anger be appeased.

Before me God stands, and the Guru stands:
who shall I bow to with these folded hands?
This heart of mine to my Guru does incline,
who showed the way to God, oh Guru mine!

Like God, my true Guru before me does stand
and for world's possessions I've no demand.
I love him, and with my love him I meet,
and I lay my head before his blessed feet.

There are four ways one can be fortunate:
the first is worship, with mind concentrate,
and the second way is in the adoration of
Saint, third world-leaving, fourth God's Love.

Make a friend of Guru, honest, true and pure
who frees you from sorrow that you endure;
don't make friends with mean men of vice,
what do they say? To the world they entice.

When the form of the real man we assume,
God's mercy is upon us we then do presume;
but when the true Guru's mercy we win,
real renunciation's love does then enter in.


The pious Saint has two hands like any man
and gives salvation to us as best as he can;
but Govind, unlike him, has twice two hands
and gives freely all that one ever demands.

The pious Saint is Truth to man revealed,
who shows us God's Truth usually concealed;
the one who firmly holds the light of Truth
will be at last changed into the One Truth.

In the friendly love of the Guru you live,
and all your thoughts to the Creator give;
these are occasions when life's lived best
and vanity of vanities is all of the rest.

Make friends with Guru honest, true, pure,
that friendship yields best fruits, be sure;
the iron over to the magic marble hold,
and see how the iron turns quickly into gold.

Make friends with Guru honest, true, pure,
that friendship yields victories, be sure;
the Bubul thorn will change to sandalwood,
none 'Nimb' will call you for you'll be good.

Lord! May Your shadow over my head remain,
and help me all of my humble hopes to gain!
I don't desire anything that's contained here
except meeting the true Guru who's so dear.

There is that Name remembered in this age;
there is also the worship of the holy Sage:
two means from endless births to be free;
keep them both in your mind with purity.

DO you travelling to Jagannath desire to go,
or to Muttra or Dwarka? Say, fool, why so?
For you cannot be unshackled from your sin
without the Saint's advice, and God within.

The true Saint does put us in God's memory,
all day by us that Name can't forgotten be;
it gives us cupfuls of that juice so divine,
which is extracted from Love's sweet wine.

What're the attributes of Saints? Just hear!
Compassion and humbleness and love sincere,
of all and not of self, and peace of mind,
being prepared to suffer pain of any kind.

His peace of **mind** the Saint does not leave,
he cares not for world's glories to receive;
insult doesn't shake him, and he has crossed
life's sea, and teeth of death has smashed.

Saint has crushed all hopes and Maya ground
and with want of Self, knowledge has found;
he doesn't know what is gladness or grief,
in mean words his lips do not find relief.


I wandered on **huge** mountains and high hills
in the pursuit of God, in fields and valleys;
I did not find Him; but when I met His man,
oh there was God, there, in a moment's span.

**8 5**

A smallest drop can be contained in the sea,
that we all do know, that's not a mystery;
but, one we call hero is one who does know
how in one small drop the whole sea to draw.

Sing of the Guru inside your constant heart;
don't let your fixed thoughts from him part;
and so you will from all the cycles be free
of birth, and you will sit in Love's eternity.

Worms of doubt eat up all mankind as well
as time, none having strength to them repel;
but, there's one: who hears the Guru's word
will have doubts taken like grain by a bird.

Curse on that life, that life that wasted is
without Highest Love: in worldly businesses,
far from the Saint like the beast irrational,
without Love he rises, but then does fall!

Have you met Guru? You have met the Lord!
It is unfathomed treasure no one has stored;
your evil thoughts will change at sight alone
and mind will adopt perfection's honest tone.

When you've met that light of Guru's face,
remember that you've seen God in his place;
the light will burn the endless sins of you
in thoughts, speech, deed, Eternity through.

Adore that true Saint who is a second Deity
because there, all true adoration does lie;
if with water you saturate all the roots,
all will thrive: branches, leaves and fruits.


If anyone does land of the true Gurus know
and does inhabit it, then surely he'll throw
aside his crowish blackness and he will be
a swan; from low he'll rise to high degree.

The Guru has all things that you can state;
go, take from him whatever is in your fate;
give up to him your mind in its entirety,
and bow down to his word in all humility.

The Guru is our second God; and so adore
the Guru, be he speechless or dumb or more,
or unfit to teach according to your thought;
if you are wise, then trust to him your lot.

That man does the highest happiness acquire
who acts up to all the teachings of his Sire.
In that One the fire of the passions dies,
god of death daring not to touch him, flies.

I Kabir say this: for you that day is great
on which you a holy Sadhu happen to meet;
fill your eyes with his light most serene,
and all your sins will be washed away, clean.

In Guru the form of great God does shine;
between these two is no distinction line;
the Sadhu and the Lord are one though two;
in all, they both the same Path do pursue.

The pupilship of the true Sages is a bliss
so much greater than all worldly happiness;
the white bird by the lake of Man is a swan
and all else cranes: so see wherever you can.

The Sages are like the trees of sandalwood,
this world's like a poisonous serpent: lewd,
it twines around the tree in poison's fire,
until by the coolness it meets its desire.

The Sages give us happiness that is sublime,
the wicked prompt us to commit sin, crime;
you, serve the Guru, oh man with open eyes:
your life's purpose will be gained. Arise!

I thank God, because such a Guru have I
that taught by him and fed by him was I;
who will now my harmless name scandalize,
free from all racial, friendly, homely ties?

My dear Saint is honest and brave and true,
he has uprooted my sorrows, not only a few;
the blacksmith the iron thread has purified
by heating, beating this and then that side.

The Guru was once greatly pleased with me
and he counselled me then in that ecstasy;
clouds of Love rained drenching on my head,
and in God's Grace all the self was washed.

Hail! All Glory be to my Guru who is great,
whose miraculous strength does many treat,
and in the twinkling of only a moment's eye
turns a beastly man into one who's heavenly.

My humble and true Guru, he advises that I
should bow before the Sages, but they deny
this honour, and they send me back to him;
their double worship shows me God Supreme.

Life, youth, greatness, all don't live forever
and nothing is eternal, no never, no never;
but to attain the fruits of this life's stage,
oh daily go, and be an associate of the Sage.

I called upon the Name of God and yet found
Him not, so in deepest grief I was drowned;
and then, I the pupilship of Sages sought,
and then suddenly the Light of Heaven got.

You who are bound to your Karma, try to be
in his hands who is now Karma-bound free;
fool, make friends of one in chains unbound,
and soon the joy of life you'll have found.

One who had half-knowledge, the false Guru,
gave to his pupil only half-knowledge too;
the little knowledge knocks about the door
with yellow robe, but receives alms no more.

Therefore mortal, test well your Guru first,
follow him who shows path to all who thirst
and he'll take you over to that other shore
and in the mirror God he'll bring you before.

There's no complete happiness for humankind
in all the worlds: no blessing is assigned;
the true happiness does only in devotion lie
and also living in the true Saints society.

The true Sadhu is a river that is tided by
the water that is the sweetest of the Deity;
bathe clean your body in it and then be sure
and your self will also be clean and pure.

Consider the moment that's the most benign,
when on you light of the Guru does shine;
for, then your lips Truth's Name will say
which will cure your life by its bright ray.

Sight of Guru will give your eyes delight
and you'll see him many times day and night
and the mercy that from there will rain
will cause you      countless profits to gain.

Only onefold is the fruit of your pilgrimage,
but fourfold is that of Guru's counsel sage,
I Kabir, say he who finds Guru who is true,
manifold fruits become what are his due.

The world complains that it is in distress;
when enjoying itself it cries in happiness;
this slave Kabir is very unhappy and cries
that it may be saved from all its miseries.

A thousand dogs snap at the dead man's bone
and snapping, fight until they're all undone;
even so does man in the broad field of life
fight for self-bliss and perish in the strife.

There's no happiness in day or in the night,
and there is none in the shadow or sunlight;
in resignation there lies the true happiness,
resign to God and those men of Saintliness.


Without Guru do not expect wisdom's light,
without him past and future are out of sight
and without him life's doubts still remain.
Success to the Guru! Long may Guru reign!

Don't expect wisdom's light without the Guru
and don't seek redemption without the Guru;
without him, no one can to us Truth explain;
without him, all our faults uncured remain.

The Guru, he is the form of God in this life
so hear him and end all of your inner strife.
He's a ladder to God by which one can go,
so hear him and then end all your woe.

Never ending is the glory of the Guru true,
and boundless are all his blessings on you;
he opens wide the Secret that's limitless,
and he leads us to the inmost lands of bliss.


Survey the seven isles and all of those nine
vast continents, and go up the worlds divine
and the upper and inner earths inspect,
yet, none true like the Guru you'll detect.

God and the Guru are really one, this I say,
by worship of Guru you really to God pray.
In life, when death does come, oh do believe
that with eyes God's Light you'll perceive.

When you've died in your past lives, the god
of death drove you from Heaven with a rod
along and across kingdoms numbered four:
you couldn't yourself to Divine love restore.

You would've wandered in the kingdoms four,
you would not have a way to Heaven's door
had not the Guru freed you from all pain
of cycle of birth and death, again and again.

God's great mercy descended on you, and so
you met the true Guru, yet, you mortal, oh
when his light of knowledge falls upon you,
you then forget him out of your vanity too.

I thank you God, that to the true Guru You
did lead my steps and I know something now.
That knowledge did reveal that You do dwell
like pearl within the cover of this shell.

You meet God if His Saint you've grasped;
tell to him your tale from first to last;
however, if the Sadhu's breath you do evade
you shall away from great God be ever laid.

Drink deep the Guru's light with your eye,
and please treat him with true hospitality;
the harder you serve him well for his bliss
the better; worse, if you gape in idleness.

A moment, sir, yes only half a moment, sir,
not even that, only half of that, I declare,
passed in the Guru's presence will save you
from many sins which may come from you.

Out of honest adoration of the true Sage
God's shown to you, hidden through the age;
and you'll be free from all sins of thought,
of speech, of deed and misery of your lot.

Too thin is the way that to God does lead,
as narrow as tenth part of a mustard seed;
when mind feeds fat on the world like a hill
how can it cross the Path, if ever it will?

Take the one-twentieth part of mustard over
and divide the twentieth into twenty more;
the mind needs contraction as small as this,
if it does desire to attain God (Jagish).

In thoughts of God alone my mind does roll,
one thought of God alone has held my soul,
one thought, no second in the inward space;
then why do I need bow low in this case?

Oh Kabir! Sing of great Govind constantly,
the mind sweet and steady in His ecstasy;
that alone is the way, try a million more,
and the mind unsteady never finds the door.

Worse than black poison is a bitter speech
from where destruction's fire to all reach;
the Sadhu speaks words that're full of bliss,
from where reigns life's honeyed happiness.

Speak the word that doesn't anything create
but love and kindness, not of spite or hate;
the real meaning of the speech there lies,
where not anger but sweet peace does rise.

One Word from the Guru's lips does rise,
but in that one Word, infinite meaning lies;
most learned saints or crammers of the Book
in vain for the inward meaning they look.

Without that Word the mind remains blind;
man knows not by what way God he will find
for closed are gates of that Word's mystery,
and man spins upon life's wheel eternally.

Yes, let wandering mind run far and wide,
but, to the Central Name you pull it aside;
whose self is steady, though mind does rove,
is not debarred, dismissed from God's Love.

The bliss given by this Illusion lasts no more
oh you foolish bliss-pursuer, than days four;
it's a dream, your kingdom and your wealth
they fly away, oh worshipper of your self!

This Illusion is a tree with branches three:
three: unhappiness and pain and also misery;
of peace under its shade no one ever dreams
for its fruit's tasteless, with disease teems.

Oh Kabir! This damsel fascinates us most,
we try and find her, then she's quickly lost;
she lives with us, with us, with us she lives
until self-control our renunciation gives.

Illusion's like a female snake, we her brood;
as snake her young, she makes us her food;
no catcher of this snake the earth has found
to catch her, twist her, to wheel her around.

Your passion does mostly to water compare,
your mind likened to salt deceit does share;
when once the lump of salt does sink below,
will you find any piece dissolved? No, no!

If mind does wish to wander then let it go;
but, don't let the body go: there is woe;
how can the arrow possibly reach its mark,
while bow-string isn't joined with the arch.

The body is like temple and mind like flag,
that in fluttering, wind's of passion wag;
he loses all his property and all his wealth,
who lets the mind at will govern the self.

# DIVAN of HAFIZ

HAFIZ was born in Shiraz, Persia (Iran) in A.D. 1320 and died there in 1389. He is considered by many of the world's great poets, mystics and writers to have been the greatest poet who has ever lived. The book that he gave to the world, his 'Divan' has been loved by millions of people of the East and the West for the past 700 years and is used as an oracle and spiritual guide by many, even today. Hafiz is not only a unique and great poet; he is also a Perfect Master, a God-realized soul whose wisdom and insights into the everyday and the mystical path are such that it is said that by reading his work one can gain spiritual advancement. His book is for everyone because he speaks as one who has gone through it all, from the passion of human love into the arms of the Divine.

This is the only modern complete English version of his book. The spiritual content is here in plain English: also the form, length of line and rhyme-structure has been achieved for the first time. In the Introduction, his life story is told in more detail than anywhere else in English. His spirituality is explored, his influence on the East and the West, the form and function of his poetry and the use of his book as a guide. Included are notes to the poems, a concordance with other English translations, a glossary, two bibliographies.

## English version by
## Paul Smith

Volume One: The Poems. 704 pages, 793 poems.
Volume Two: The Introduction. 256 pages. Full color Persian miniatures on covers. 10" X 7", Clothbound. Limited Ed. 1000.
A SUPERB QUALITY BOOK PRODUCTION***************************
ISBN   0 949191 00 0     USA $65.00, AUST. $79.00, U.K. £48.00

# STAY WITH GOD
## Francis Brabazon

"...modern mystical epic" Annemarie Schimmel, Prof. of Indo-Muslim studies at Harvard and author of many books on Eastern Poetry and Religion.

ILLUSTRATED BY JOHN PARRY, THIRD EDITION, 174 PAGES........
8 1/2" X 5 1/2 " PERFECTBOUND, Full-color Cover. USA $11.95
ISBN   0 949191 07 8         AUST. $15.95        U.K. £7.50

# HAFIZ Tongue of the Hidden

## POEMS FROM THE DIVAN

*Versions by Paul Smith*

Decorations by Dale Hickey

Hafiz was not only (along with Rumi) considered Persia's greatest poet, and by Goethe and Emerson and many others... the greatest poet who ever lived, but he was also considered to be the greatest writer of ghazals: a form of mystical love poetry. Here is a selection of sixty-two of his best ghazals from his great work, the Divan. Included is a long Introduction on his life and times, on his spirituality, on his poetry (including the ghazal) and a glossary.

8 1/2" X 5 1/2" perfectbound, 96 pages, ill.,     USA $8.95
ISBN  0 949191 05 1     AUST. $12.95     U.K. £6.00

# BURNING ILLUSION
## Poems by David Stewart

To build mansions of feeling with hovel words
For You, the impossible desire, strange:
To wield the blade of intellect in hearts herds
Finding You the Friend, though out of range
Is my work in verse. You the secret hand
Are the destiny and guiding force grand.

Here are the poems of someone who has been to hell and has come back, spent some time doing purgatory and has now placed his feet firmly on this earth and has tied his future to a star that shines heavenwards. These are brave poems: original, searching, sometimes demanding, literate, loving, longing, but above all, unforgetably human.

8 1/2" X 5 1/2" perfectbound, 96 pages.     USA $6.95
ISBN  0 949191 06 X     AUST. $9.95     U.K. £4.50

# BOOK OF THE WINEBRINGER

# Masnavi of Hafiz
### Versions by Paul Smith

The masnavi is the form used in Persian poetry to write epic ballads or spiritual romances. Each couplet has a different rhyme. This is to allow the poet greater freedom. All the great long narrative poems were composed in this form which is a Persian invention. The most famous poems written in this form were by Rumi, Nizami, Jami and of course, Hafiz. 'The Book of the Winebringer', 'The Wild Deer', and 'The Book of the Minstrel' by Hafiz, are all considered to be masterpieces and also included in this collection are his other masnavi.

8 1/2" X 5 1/2" illustrated, 96 pages, perfectbound    USA $8.95
ISBN   0 949191 03 5         AUST. $12.95         U.K.   £6.00

# LOVE'S PERFECT GIFT

# Rubaiyat of Hafiz
### Versions by Paul Smith

The ruba'i is a poetic form already known in the West because of the 'Rubaiyat of Omar Khayyam' which contains many ruba'is of Hafiz and other Persian poets, being an anthology of such poems collected down the ages. FitzGerald the great translator of Omar says of Hafiz: "The best Musician of Words".

> O my Beloved. while this life of mine I can be offering
> To soft down of Your cheek: I can never be leaving.
> For my soul's sweet nourishment, for Your lip's ruby,
> Two hundred thousand jewels I would never be taking.

This is the largest collection of Hafiz's ruba'is ever published in English: 147 poems. The correct rhyme-structure and form has been kept throughout... the result of seven years work. "Paul Smith has achieved a remarkable feat... an inexhaustible well of inspired images..." The Age.

"Hafiz is as highly esteemed by his countrymen as Shakespeare by us, and deserves as serious consideration" A.J. Arberry.

8 1 2" X 5 1/2" perfectbound, illustrated.         USA $8.95
ISBN   0 949191 04 3   96 pages.    AUST. $12.95, U.K.   6.00